Unwin Education Books
Teaching Today: 3

The Use of Resources

JOHN HANSON

The Use of Resources

JOHN HANSON

Foreword by James Porter
Principal, Berkshire College of Education

London
GEORGE ALLEN & UNWIN LTD
Ruskin House   Museum Street

ISBN 0 04 371027 1 hardback
ISBN 0 04 371028 X paperback

Printed in Great Britain
in Times Roman type
by Cox & Wyman Ltd,
London, Fakenham and Reading

Foreword

It is a great pleasure to write the foreword to this contribution to the *Teaching Today* series.

As the James Committee's Report on Teacher Education and Training indicated, 'The best education and training of teachers is that which is built upon and illuminated by a growing maturity and experience.' John Hanson's book will make a particular contribution to such further education and training of teachers. Too many educational texts become locked in vague generalisations or are becalmed in detail unrelated to objectives. Also, many others have accepted the ideas of student-centred education but failed to appreciate the complex skills and knowledge needed to sustain such an enterprise. This book, and others in the *Teaching Today* series demonstrate the way in which a humane and sensitive emphasis upon the experience of student learning can be combined with a highly practical and well organised management of appropriate resources.

The Use of Resources begins with the bold assertion that 'All the world's a resource' and proceeds to establish the criteria for selecting and designing resources for learning and teaching in school. Drawing on a deep appreciation of recent examples of curriculum innovation and published advice to teachers, it establishes arguments for resource-based learning which provide a succinct rationale for practice in the classroom. Objectives are always linked to actual examples of work with children, and many contain ideas which will be new to those in school. Most of them can easily be adapted to varying school situations. For those who are looking for ways of handling the bewildering array of material now available there is wise and balanced advice. This is true whether it is concerned with deciding on the size of paper or with explaining the mysteries of OCCI, the optical-coincidence index.

Mr Hanson's book ends as it begins with an emphasis upon the human resource of teachers and students, for, as he argues, 'It is in the quality of their experience, their ideas and their response that our ultimate success or failure will be judged.' The book should be read not only by those who use resources but also those such as local authority administrators, who are responsible for providing some of the funds, as among other clear messages coming from the book there is an indication that teachers require adequate time, money and ancillary help to select, collate and handle such an important development, and to give greater reality to our assertions about the growth of independent learning and the provision of more comprehensive education. Given such support, Mr Hanson's book greatly enlarges the prospect of the ultimate success of such a development.

JAMES PORTER

Contents

Chapter 1

The Present Situation

Anything used to meet an educational need might be called a 'resource' – buildings, staff, equipment, ideas and material. In practice these are interrelated. This book, however, is concerned chiefly with the information and materials required for teaching and learning.

We hear much now about 'resources for learning'. If we want to draw the distinction between teaching and learning this phrase puts the emphasis in the right place. Perhaps the Arabs were wiser in deriving both their words from the same root.

There is a distinction to be drawn between materials ('software') and the equipment ['hardware'] which may be needed to project or transmit them. We are more conscious today of the media or means by which information is conveyed. The main types of media existed in the last century but the choices open to teachers were more limited. There were books, of course, but the blackboard as a visual aid and the teacher's voice as an audio aid had little competition. The environment beyond the classroom was hidden from view, for the windows were set high, drawing the children's eyes heavenward.

Is there a danger that, with the attractive aids now available (for example the multi-media kits which include a variety of different materials in one package), we may overlook the real things that exist within our reach? The hedge round the school field, the town street, the people in the community, the clay that may lie beneath the soil – all of these are resources.

All the world's a resource. And the sheer profusion makes it the more essential that we adopt sound criteria in selecting resources and designing them. To establish those criteria is no easy task for it demands of us a critical awareness of what happens when children learn and of what we want of education and life. As we use more resources we need good management techniques in handling, storing and retrieving them. This book will examine these topics.

Our ideas and circumstances are of course constantly changing. We are no longer required, like the eighteenth-century schoolmaster, to be 'orthodox for religion and of godly conversation', qualified to teach the Latin and Greek tongues and entitled to charge an extra fee 'if thought fit to teach English'. Nor must we promise, like the North Carolina schoolmistress, 'not to go out with any young man except in so far as it may be necessary to stimulate Sunday school work'. Greater professional freedom has however surely brought with it an obligation to exercise a greater professional judgement.

To discuss resources is to ask questions about educational aims, objectives, methods and outcomes. At the end we might decide that our main strength lies in our own resourcefulness and that of our students.

THE POSITION

An increasing teacher involvement

The teacher who relies exclusively on didactic methods in their most passive form has a very limited need for resources. He sits or stands at his desk, with blackboard, chalk and red pencil to hand, and providing that the students apply themselves diligently to their class textbook, then indeed,

> 'God's in his Heaven
> All's right with the world.'

His modest demands of a termly box of chalks and a new set of the same textbook after eight years will not cause financial embarrassment.

While such stereotypes do exist, our profession generally has always been more resourceful. Over the past ten years, moreover, there have been a number of developments which have increased the ways in which we obtain, make and use learning materials. One of the most important developments has been the greater involvement of teachers in the preparation of new courses and resources.

The process of reappraising, designing, testing and evaluating methods, courses and materials is curriculum development. We may consider this in terms of curriculum renewal, which is bringing ideas up to date, or curriculum innovation, which implies testing ourselves in new situations and is more likely to arouse controversy. We still understand too little of the management processes needed to encourage innovation within our schools.

Over the past ten years a new range of resources has become available locally and nationally as a result of curriculum innovation.

Teachers have never lacked advice and criticism but they were generally able to point out to their learned critics that 'theory without practice is sterile'. However, the curriculum development movement powered by the Schools Council and the Nuffield Foundation was based on projects committed to the design and publication of new materials tested in school situations. Lawrence Stenhouse pointed out, at the 1973 North of England Conference, 'It demands that ideas be translated into action, that educational thought should accept the discipline of practice, and practise the leaven of critical thinking.'[1]

Not all teachers have exercised their professional freedom to examine critically and respond to those ideas and materials. Some have waited for manna to fall from above and accepted it without much consideration for its objectives and implications. Others have been denied access to ideas and materials because of the high cost of some project materials or because of shortcomings in the system, such as it existed, for making information available. Nevertheless, it was suggested, secondary education had been made pregnant by artificial dissemination.

A wider co-operation

It was once generally accepted as the responsibility of the individual teacher to devise his or her scheme of work or follow that laid down by the head of department or head teacher. The development of team teaching since 1960 has led to more co-operative planning and work preparation. Many schools have recognised the value of this by timetabling team planning periods.

In some parts of Britain groups of schools have been encouraged by their Local Authority to work together on curriculum development projects. Leicestershire, Shropshire, Oxfordshire and ILEA were among the early Authorities promoting local co-operation and involvement, and more recently Bristol (Avon).

Secondary reorganisation has been another factor promoting co-operation between schools. Schools being merged or linked have been obliged to put their heads together. This has sometimes had a detrimental effect: a rigid doctrine has been established by a 'senior' school over its neighbours, resulting in educational *'rigor mortis'*. I think difficulties are more likely to arise where links demanding co-operation are imposed from 'above' without consultation with all staff. An acknowledged need for sound links between different levels, for instance between primary schools and the secondary school(s) to which they contribute children, has led to better communication and occasionally to a genuine cross-fertilisation.

The role of the CSE examination in the widening participation of teachers in curriculum development should not be overlooked. In the Southern Board region, for example, the Integrated Studies panel, which for seven years considered and moderated courses of an interdisciplinary nature, stimulated many schools to consider in depth their methods and objectives. Mode III gave teachers the chance to exercise initiative.

The expansion of curriculum development at national level, chiefly through the Schools Council, and a consequent need for local dissemination, brought teachers' centres into existence. It was envisaged that these centres would bring teachers into contact with national projects and materials and also stimulate 'grass roots' activity. Schools Council projects expressed a hope that teachers would adapt materials to suit their local situation. By 1972 most Local Authorities had created teachers' centres. A number of these flourished and became resource centres for the schools they served. Others languished for want of ideas, facilities and leadership. 'Modified rapture'.

Have we got our priorities right?

A great wealth of fresh ideas and resources became available to teachers through Schools Council projects. The Schools Council has been criticised on the ground that its projects, normally at national level with teams linked to a relatively small number of trial schools and in a few cases reluctant to release information or materials before their commercial publication, may have inhibited rather than stimulated professional initiatives. A few of the later projects, such as the Mathematics for the Majority continuation project, have set out from the start to engage groups of local teachers in the making of materials. The Schools Council gave its support to the North-west Project in which a considerable number of teachers' centres worked jointly, following the original lead from Dr Alan Rudd of Manchester University, to produce resources for the raising of the school leaving age.

Have 'grass roots' developments received sufficient encouragement? Should there be more co-ordination to promote regional projects?

Will the implementation of the James Proposals and the new opportunities available to us just result in more 'chalk and talk' inservice training? In recent years there has been a shift in both LEA and DES courses towards 'workshop' courses and practical work on resources. It is no longer true that we go to curriculum development to do and to inservice training to be done. But have we yet got our priorities in balance?

It has been said that 'we only understand fully those things which we have done ourselves'. The Nuffield 5–13 Mathematics Project found in Tavistock Square a Chinese proverb: 'I hear and I forget, I see and I remember, I do and I understand.' Is that true of us as teachers? How important is it that we ourselves should be involved in the hammering-out of better courses and resources? There are observers, of course, who allege that just as we expect too much from children in terms of initiative and originality (an allegation which many primary school teachers would reject), so we demand too much from teachers in general. Do we deserve our professional freedom?

The primary school 'revolution'

Another significant factor in the changing resources situation is the wider use of mixed ability grouping and more active learning methods in which students are given direct access to resources. It may be summed up as a move towards more individualised learning.

Theories, advanced with evidence by psychologists such as Piaget of how children learn, were seized upon by teachers who felt that traditional, authoritarian teaching methods were inadequate. Opportunities were taken to introduce 'progressive' methods into infant and primary schools. These methods were 'child-centred' and allowed children to develop more as individuals and at their own pace. They were to let children learn in a natural way and to harness their many changing interests. As comprehensive reorganisation removed the constraints of the 11 + examination, many more primary schools in some Authority areas went over to this approach. Class lessons, rows of desks, timetabled subjects and the teacher at the front were replaced by group activity, the organisation of the classroom into work bays, the 'integrated day' and the teacher everywhere to give help when needed, being like the Good Lord 'slow to chide and swift to bless'. Resources were put around the children without imposing rigid lines of study but the main emphasis was on exploiting children's interests, and experience through the local environment, the richest resource of all.

The arguments for modern primary education were given at length in the Plowden Report *Children and their Primary Schools*.[2] Critics suggested that its recommendations were not based on concrete evidence. A more typical criticism came from C. M. Johnson, writing on 'Freedom in Primary Schools' in the first Black Paper:[3] 'The world is a noisy, chaotic and restless place, yet in schools we see the same lack of quiet being encouraged. It is putting a great strain on young children to leave them constantly to make decisions with rarely any time in the day when they are quiet and listening.' But Margaret Drabble began a thoughtful article in *The Times*: 'The excellence of our primary education is widely acknowledged. Most children expect to enjoy primary school, and do. I asked a child last week how his school day had been, and he said "Lovely", as though this were a natural response.'

Each of us will have a view on this issue and may see in a school only what confirms our own prejudices. Research results always seem capable of manipulation, and an elderly member of staff in the corner of the room is bound to observe that he saw all these new ideas when he started teaching thirty-nine years ago, and then put forward the theory of educational cycles. It may be that we are all born as cavaliers or roundheads – teachers of children or teachers of subjects. How objective can we be? The debate continues: Is the aim of education to acquire knowledge or is knowledge a means of education?

Educational methods, and the resources designed to support them, are based on value systems, though the values are hidden. This raises questions which may carry important implications for education in developing countries. Should, for example, teachers encourage independent, questioning methods among children in a community where parents still exercise a strict authority in line with the values of the traditional culture?

Changes in secondary education

While the debate continued on primary education, attempts were made from 1965 onward to introduce less authoritarian methods into secondary schools. Enquiry-based and individualised learning became objectives shaping Schools Council projects. A team led by Charity James at Goldsmith's College stimulated a number of schools to experiment with 'interdisciplinary enquiry'[4] but the resources to sustain this approach were not produced. Attempts in the past to introduce individualised learning in a systematic way, the most ambitious venture of which was the Dalton Plan in America, have failed to gain a wide and lasting hold. Nevertheless, a number of more modest schemes within schools have been successful and Local Authorities have in some areas anticipated further development by designing more open-planned buildings. Prestigious new schools have dedicated themselves to less authoritarian methods and an imaginative use of resources. L. C. Taylor, in his book *Resources for Learning*,[5] has acknowledged the shortcomings of earlier efforts towards individualised learning but argued strongly that we must prepare to try again.

An interesting outcome of the movement to enliven the first years of comprehensive schooling has been the creation of the 8–12 and 9–13 middle schools.[6] Some Authorities saw this as an educational need and approached the problem with enthusiasm and imagination. Here was the means of extending the best of primary school practice and achieving continuity of approach across the middle years of schooling with a continuing, close relationship between child and teacher. It must be added that a few Authorities adopted middle schools as an administrative expediency.

Some of the problems arising

Secondary schools developing more active methods have met problems. One of these has arisen from the team teaching and planning which has initially stimulated teachers to prepare new courses with great energy and drive. At the end of about three years, however, the team can find that, while new methods have been established, the investment in particular resources mitigates against further change. The excitement is partly lost and new members of staff cannot be involved in the same way. Consistent development is difficult to sustain in a school situation.

Problems can result from our limited knowledge of how students learn by enquiry. As a general method, is it more suited to students at a particular age? Is it more appropriate for certain levels of ability? Can it be that different students learn most effectively by different educational methods? In my experience it is frequently the teachers most successful with enquiry methods who ask these questions.

Methods are seldom changed over a whole school. Changes tend to occur in one or two departments, and often then at one age level, simply because of the work load involved. To what extent are our students aware of inconsistencies? Does it matter?

Good ideas can be aborted by the manner in which change is attempted. How often have teachers lacking conviction been cajoled into co-operating with eager colleagues? How often has the head teacher imposed a new scheme? A very experienced teacher told me recently of his experiences with a team using the Schools Council Humanities materials. He was not disturbed so much by the incident in which he had a toe-to-toe shouting match with a young mistress in front of the class on a matter of birth control and women's rights (he didn't go much for neutrality anyway), but he had very reluctantly agreed with the head of department to take the course into the following year, and it was not until the new term started that he realised that the head of department himself had opted out, not wishing to be involved in the actual teaching of it. Attitudes are at the core of our professional problem.

Research projects have not so far been very convincing in the evaluation of specific methods and resources. Educational research often offers us fine descriptions rather than scientific evidence. School situations contain many variable factors. We seem to do best when we are convinced that the methods we are employing are right. Maintaining a critical awareness is an important aspect of our professional role.

A resources explosion

A growing acceptance of enquiry methods which give students more frequent access to a wider range of resources has created an additional demand for resources. So, frequently, has the introduction of mixed ability grouping. Other factors have also contributed to this greater demand: optional courses in the Fourth and Fifth Years of the secondary school, the raising of the school leaving age and the idea of educating for future leisure have helped to broaden the curriculum and promoted new courses.

Commercial publishers, though hesitant to invest in *avant-garde* ideas, have moved to meet this demand, supplementing and sometimes competing with the materials published on behalf of Nuffield and Schools Council projects. Organisations with vested interests and crusading ideas in education are offering material to schools. So the catalogues, fat and thin, glossy and duplicated, plain and coloured, pour into our schools day by day.

At another level, advances at the frontiers of knowledge influence the curriculum in our schools. Those who extend or reshape human knowledge oblige us sooner or later to reconsider our own ground, though we may be no more aware of their probing than of Auden's 'weary Asia tugging gently at the night'. We tire of being told that knowledge is doubling every two, three or four years [the claims vary], but knowledge is no longer a stable element. We need to renew our resources more frequently to keep up to date.

Think too of the advances in technology that have made new equipment available to us, if we can afford it. New machines imply a new format for materials, even though the subject content may remain unchanged. Whiteboard competes with blackboard, and the overhead projector with both. We could draw up a very impressive list of aids, including the videotape-recorder which has probably trebled the use of televised broadcasts in schools. Multi-media kits can be bought from commercial publishers who a few years ago traded only in books. How far away is computer-based learning? So, it is not only that a greater weight of resources exists – they exist in a wider range of media.

Our schools are facing a log jam of information and materials. Decisions are harder to make. How can we find out what is immediately available to us? How can we quickly discover the sources and materials economically? Can we store what we find and find what we store? Such questions have prompted a fresh interest in management techniques.

Valuable equipment is not being used economically in some schools. Can we justify a slide-projector or tape-recorder lying idle in a departmental cupboard because no one else knows it is there or because the department is reluctant to loan it (sometimes with good reasons)? Videotape-recorders may be little used because a school did not realise the cost of videotape, no one is available to operate it when needed, or because the recording point is too far away from the aerial relay unit to receive a good signal.

One of the most costly aids of all is the language laboratory and evidence so far of its effectiveness in schools is rather disappointing. Have the needs for technical assistance to maintain the equipment been sufficiently considered by schools and their Authorities? Have language teachers the time and inclination to prepare resources additional to the packaged course? May other departments justify use of the lab? We may move towards a more flexible use of such facilities by which the lab can be split up and moved around the school to meet smaller group needs as they arise. Mobile mini-labs are already in operation. Traditional methods made fewer demands on us.

Producing resources within schools

Schools now produce themselves more of the materials they need. Some might trace this trend back to the decision to raise the school leaving age and to the Newsom Report *Half Our Future*, which was a significant publication although its terms of reference did not include methods and materials; indeed, the report made no real reference to 'resources'. Our present emphasis on resources should not obscure the more fundamental questions on attitudes to young people and their learning which was the report's great strength.

The 'do-it-yourself' approach to educational materials has arisen mainly in the information subjects (Social Studies, Geography, History, etc.) and in courses not governed by external examining bodies. In some cases there has been genuine renewal and innovation; in others it has been an exercise with scissors and photocopier.

An early result of these initiatives in many schools has been frustration with the school office, which was not planned to cope with these new demands. A range of needs has been revealed: more secretarial and ancillary staff, a room efficiently laid out for printing or duplicating, facilities for recording tape live and off-air, a darkroom, and good reprographic equipment.

The traditional school library has found difficulty in reacting to independent study methods and librarians have been hesitant to handle non-book materials.

The development of resource centres

The resource centre movement, which gained momentum in the early 1970s, aimed to remedy these deficiencies. The school resource centre, it was argued, could be organised and staffed to classify, index and store materials in a business-like manner. It could be responsible for locating sources and information and for obtaining further materials as needs were expressed. Served by an adjacent reprographic unit it could produce and reproduce items, while a maintenance and loan service could see to equipment which no department could justify retaining for full-time use. The centre, serving every department and stimulating curriculum development, would encourage co-operation and harmony.

To some this came as a vision of an educational Harrods on their own premises, a treasure cave to which every educational need would be an 'Open Sesame'. The movement had an American inspiration but we should not be deluded by travellers' tales and pictures of magnificent resource centres into thinking that this is the common situation in the United States; in fact a great many American teachers have never seen nor used such a centre. But a vision is there.

At the other extreme sceptics have seen no reason for school resource centres, regarding them as the latest fad and a threat to their departmental autonomy. K. Evans, in '*Secondary Education*',[8] added his cautionary note: 'It would be an unmitigated tragedy if the fate of the new media were to mirror that of the old: centralised, classified, catalogued – and marginal to learning.'

Parallel with experiments at school level, pilot schemes to produce and disseminate resources at Authority and regional level have been established; for example, by the Exeter Regional Resource Centre, Wiltshire, Oxfordshire, Leicestershire, Dumbarton and ILEA. Local-government reorganisation may have given a further spur to this trend, while the Committee for Educational Technology has undertaken feasibility studies in cataloguing and computer-storing national AVA collections.[9]

Are we moving towards a more rationalised system by which information on sources and resources can be networked and standardised procedures adopted for handling it?

Difficult economic conditions and continuing paper shortages may lead to new forms of collaboration between LEAs and publishers. Materials seen and ordered at final trial stage by teachers, through their LEA, could be obtained, by bulk contract, at considerably reduced costs.

Chapter 2
Criteria for Selecting and Designing Resources

PLANNING

Aims

Our planning and rethinking often start formally from a consideration of aims and objectives. What are we trying to do? Why?

Some teachers claim that aims and objectives are not so vital
to planning and should be forged in the heat of developing a new
course or activity, or be implicit in our actions. Robin Hodgkin in
his paper 'The Qualitative Element'[10] suggests that both aims and
shorter-term objectives are 'essentially trivial' and that quality
comes from the *work* of attaining them. To some even planning, in
the sense of imposing a structure on the child's learning, is un-
desirable and they may take literal comfort from Cromwell's remark
that 'none goes so far as he who knows not whither he goeth'. The
most child-centred aims suggest that resources should be dictated
by the needs of the moment, not determine them.

Dewey reminded teachers many years ago that education itself has
no aims, 'only persons, parents and teachers have aims'. When defined, they are often in vague, affective terms such as 'to develop
sound attitudes'. Thinking about educational aims is rather like
thinking about the purpose of life – we utter very generalised state-
ments. We may do so with conviction and faith, but our broadest
aims may be no more than woolly blankets to insulate us from cold
reality. Even so they will indicate certain attitudes towards resources.

Our aims, and hence attitudes towards resources, need to reflect
our situation. Thus the Secondary School Social Science Project
in Papua and New Guinea states that 'a course in social education
in Papua–New Guinea must be concerned with social change'. In
the United States, Miller's survey[11] of aims stated in History textbooks between 1888 and 1927 showed 'To discipline the mind' as
the clear favourite. Big changes in American society in the first
decades of this century led to 'Educating for democracy' topping the
poll for the period up to 1958. Since then the trend has been towards

behavioural goals and more specific understandings. One of the aims of 'Man – A Course of Study', a project directed by Bruner, is 'to instil concern for the human condition in all its forms, whatever race or culture'.

Aims identify our ground and give points of reference to those around us. The Humanities Project directed by Lawrence Stenhouse has the stated aim 'to develop understanding of social situations and human acts and of the controversial issues which they raise'.[12] It reflects perhaps a current mood for social introspection. Few teachers would argue against such an aim, though the discussion methods and teacher role advocated by the Project to achieve understanding did arouse some controversy.

Many primary school teachers want to express their aims in terms of the child. If, however, they speak of the child's 'educational needs', it can be argued that they are simply translating their own beliefs into child-centred terms. Aims carry a personal quality, as we should expect. In a survey conducted by Dr Dennis Lawton's 8–13 Social Studies Project,[13] it was noted that 114 primary and secondary schools had between them suggested 140 different aims for social studies. Custom cannot stale our infinite variety.

The criteria by which we should select and design resources become clearer when we consider our educational objectives. Objectives are goals which, in the shorter or longer term, we plan to achieve and towards which we can measure attainment and progress. Our objectives will cover skills and methods, knowledge and concepts, and attitudes and behaviour, though the latter can only be assessed subjectively. Before setting down objectives we need to consider carefully the nature of the learning process and the structure of knowledge.

Methods and the learning process

The main factors shaping the resources we use are the nature of the students, the subject content, and the nature of the learning process itself.

Much has been written on the subject of educational methods and the ways by which students learn. Much remains to be discovered. Bloom's *Taxonomy of Education Objectives*[14] is a standard work but a more easily digested exposition will be found in the published Teachers' Guides for some Schools Council projects – for example, the 5–13 Science Project[15] and the 8–13 History, Geography and Social Sciences Project.

The first important distinction I want to make in learning methods is between the mode of enquiry and the mode of experience. These correspond closely to Bloom's terms of cognitive and affective learning.

The mode of enquiry, which some would call the scientific method, concerns the obtaining, organising and expression of information. *The mode of experience* concerns the organisation and expression of feelings, imagination and creative ideas. Both contribute to understanding.

We may note in passing that such school subjects as Science, Geography, Mathematics and Technology are devoted chiefly to enquiry, while Art, Music, Drama and Literature centre more on experience and imagination. (Physical Education, Typing and Dance bring in a range of kinosthetic skills but these fall outside the scope of this book.)

The modes of enquiry and experience are two dimensions of the whole learning process. In both modes I would identify six elements or phases: motivation, instruction, search, problem-solving, concept-formation and presentation of work. It is difficult to find words which do not mean different things to different teachers; they require further definition.

Motivation is the catalytic agent which quickens the other phases of learning. It is therefore an important criterion in the selection of resources.

Instruction covers that phase of learning where there is a need to introduce, explain and demonstrate. It establishes the prior basis of knowledge which is the necessary foundation of enquiry.

Instruction has traditionally centred on the teacher. Wherever education was regarded as a privilege, he was accorded much respect, being recognised as a repository of knowledge and its principal medium. His dissertations and demonstrations might be challenged by his peers but not by his charges. 'And still the wonder grew, That one small head could carry all he knew.'

We live in a different world. As G. S. V. Petter HMI wrote in an article on 'Values and the Curriculum',

'Nowadays mass media, audio and visual, as well as the printed word, have dramatically changed the role of the teacher. To what extent is he or she any more the "authority" except in a titular, monitorial sense and in as much as there is some experience peculiar to the teacher that can be communicated?'

We are not yet redundant. The need for sound human relationships is perhaps stronger today than before. And is there any substitute for the good story well told or the gift of being able to inspire? Our role has certainly changed. We tend to talk with our students rather than at them. The need for them to be actively rather than passively involved is widely accepted. But what things are best 'discovered' and what best taught? What validity have the traditional methods of instruction now?

The qualities most commonly demanded by teachers in instruction are firstly, the ability to listen, look and read with attention and comprehension; and secondly, the ability to remember information.

It is when required qualities like this are converted to specific objectives for a lesson or unit of study that the choice and design of resources become critical. Resources play a large part in determining actual outcomes.

Search is the finding and recording of information or evidence, together with its interpretation and classification. By its nature, genuine search or research is inclined to be student-centred and resource-centred, and may often be most easily undertaken by individuals or small groups.

An understanding of search and problem-solving is critical to a sound curricular policy and to preparations for interdisciplinary studies. Each subject or 'discipline' has its individual mode of search and problem-solving. Thus a geologist searches for his evidence, records, interprets and organises it in a very different way from, say, an anthropologist or historian; not because the skills in principle are different but because they are being applied to different material.

When a student begins Woodwork he soon discovers that he will get results by planing along the grain but will make little progress and much firewood if he planes across the grain. He must adapt his approach to the discipline of the material. Similarly, the would-be potter, in exploring his material, succeeds by handling the clay in a particular manner. Does not the same apply to academic enquiry? We make real progress when we recognise and conform to the discipline of our material and when we adopt the language which allows us to communicate our findings.

If we accept that each true subject has its own active mode of enquiry, and indeed its own raptures, then I suggest that integration of them is not feasible. Integration is a matter of active disciplines contributing to wider problems and topics; at an organisational level it is a matter of teacher co-operation.

This concept of a discipline or subject, based on its specific methods and not just on a corporate body of knowledge, does not always conform with school subjects. History is arguably a subject by this definition, though the experience of human affairs needed for problem-solving may be possessed by few students under the age of 16. Geography can embrace a range of disciplines and may be described more accurately as a field. Advocates of broad Humanities courses can argue that their approach means not the abolition of subjects but the involvement of more (including Anthropology, Archaeology and Sociology) than were considered under the traditional time table and curriculum. Bruner's 'Man–A Course of Study' is one example of a course which introduces new disciplines into the classroom.

In the mode of experience, search represents an exploration of self, experience and emotion in order to give 'an outward expression of an inner state'.

The qualities commonly expected by teachers to arise from search studies are these:

The ability to observe and record accurately.
Knowledge of suitable sources.
The ability to handle materials and equipment competently.
The ability to follow instructions.
The ability to interpret evidence (e.g. archives, maps, graphs).
The ability to classify evidence.[16]

Again it is when these qualities are converted to specific objectives in planning a particular unit of study that the choice and design of resources become critical. The History teacher who wants his students to be able to interpret historical evidence cannot rely on a textbook which conveys only predigested information and contains no original sources. He must provide a range of suitable reference material and consider carefully what first-hand evidence is at hand in the local environment. A Drama teacher, perhaps concerned as much with experience and imagination as skills, will use a very different range of resources, including lighting effects, space and, not least, his own powers of inspiration and evocation.

Problem-solving means the handling and consideration of evidence in order to make a decision or design a solution to a practical, factual or moral problem. It requires students to evaluate evidence, propose and test hypotheses, recognise the important factors in a situation and apply their knowledge to new circumstances.

Much 'project work' and enquiry-based learning in schools stops short at searching for and finding information, which is put into poorly decorated files without any more testing assignments. Thinking about ideas and problems, and making and justifying decisions, are very much part of the full process of enquiry. It is the essence of that 'critical awareness' which is so often advocated. As H. L. Elvin claimed in *Education in Contemporary Society* in 1965, 'we have not faced the problem of giving the academically less gifted the critical awareness of society without which society must be the poorer'.

Problem-solving, in its many forms, can be encouraged within an individual discipline. Is it equally important that tribute should also be paid to wider issues? Young people do not see the world through a spectrum of curricular subjects and most of today's significant problems are interdisciplinary in character.

The qualities commonly demanded as a result of problem-solving approaches are:

The ability to evaluate evidence and data.
The ability to make an independent and group judgement.
The ability to test and justify conclusions.
Originality of thought.
The ability to apply knowledge and experience to new situations.

Concept-formation means the recognition and understanding of concepts or key ideas. In the pyramidal relationship of ideas on a topic, concepts are at the top. They enable us to organise our information on a higher level of understanding.

The learning of concepts is surely implicit in the objective of 'organising evidence and ideas'. The identification of specific concepts (e.g. interdependence) as objectives was first adopted by curriculum projects in America. The practice is now widespread. The Schools' Council 8–13 Project in History, Geography and Social Science, for example, agreed on these seven key concepts: communication; power; values and beliefs; conflict/consensus; similarity/difference; continuity/change; causality.

Concepts are helpful to planning, and the structuring of information is critical to learning, but I am not convinced that concept-formation can be phased into learning situations in the same way as search. Experience in a number of schools has suggested that resources designed simply to teach concepts are unsuccessful. This section is therefore omitted from the later chapters on resource planning.

The qualities commonly found relevant here are:

The ability to generalise.
The ability to organise evidence.
The ability to see and appreciate significant concepts.

Presentation refers to the students' own work. When they have made their decisions and considered solutions, students are normally asked to present their work and ideas to the teacher. This is an everyday feature of school life to which the exercise book has long been dedicated. Do we forget that audio-visual aids can be creative tools as well as teaching aids? Need the student always present his work with the teacher in mind? Might he not on occasions seek his peers or the local community as his audience? Indeed, if the school sees itself as a part of the community as well as a community in itself, it might consider that much excellent work put into exercise books would be better displayed at the local railway station.

The qualities sought from presentation are these:

The ability to communicate fluently and accurately.
The ability to select a suitable medium for communication.

Because the nature of learning should have a dominant part in shaping the resources we require, the later chapters dealing with the criteria for the choice and preparation of resources are based on the heading previously outlined: motivation; instruction; search; problem-solving, presentation.

However, before we consider those criteria in more detail we must take note of the relationships involved in learning activities and investigate briefly how subject content may be organised.

Relationships in learning activities

The objectives we adopt in relation to attitudes and behaviour are often tied closely to our overall aims and are difficult to assess for progress and attainment. They are important in determining how far we consciously develop social skills such as the facility to co-operate with other members of a group. Social skills have been ignored by those teachers who have relied on instructional methods and an authoritarian relationship. Clearly we must consider whether our chosen aims and objectives in behaviour and social skills are consistent with our method objectives, for conflicts could arise. Resources are involved too.

We can identify three main types of learning activity in our schools: teacher-centred, resource-centred, and student-centred. The difference between them lies in the relationship of the student to the teacher and the resources. It is a question of where authority is invested.

Teacher-centred activity places the initiative and authority firmly with the teacher to inspire interest, direct the course of study, demonstrate, explain, ask questions, issue assignments and set standards. He is active; the students are passive. He tends to have the important resources, and the students proceed at the pace he allows. Conformity is often an unwritten objective of this approach, though not necessarily an outcome. But a gifted French teacher, for example, may use an overhead projector to project cartoons which stimulate vigorous discussion, a desire to use the language and lead naturally into active role-play situations.

Resource-centred activity relies on materials designed or brought within the student's orbit to stimulate interest, instruct, raise questions, provide evidence, advise and explain. The teacher in this approach exercises, if he is present, a less direct authority, acting more often as an adviser. A high premium is placed on *individual* progress and on the ability to work independently and in small groups. Search and problem-solving obviously tend to be resource-centred.

Student-centred activity requires students to show initiative and direct their own studies, individually or co-operatively. The teacher again acts in a less authoritarian manner to earn respect. This approach demands a high level of resources and tends to diminish very structured and detailed planning.

All three types of activity may be observed within a single lesson. It is surely the mark of a good teacher that he or she knows which is the most appropriate at any time to a specific purpose.

To impose a design, pattern, sequence or structure upon educational material is to build in certain values and relationships to authority. Information can, for example, be presented in a manner which discourages questioning. If a single sheet is stapled with other sheets into book form, a fairly rigid structure results which implies a given sequence and inhibits the degree of student choice which is afforded by a folder of loose-leaf material. The form in which learning material is presented can establish a certain teacher–student relationship as firmly as the organisation of desks and tables in a classroom.

Many teachers value those raw and unstructured resources such as paint, clay and the living environment which allow the student to explore freely and individually, extend his experience and build up his own structures. Our schools have traditionally relied on the teacher as authority and instructor, but the student-centred approach now found in many primary schools is consistent with their teachers' redefined aims and behavioural objectives. With the trend towards enquiry-based learning, resource-based activity has won favour in secondary schools but attempts to introduce this approach systemati-cally, the best known probably being the Dalton Plan developed in America several decades ago,[17] have enjoyed only limited success. Student-centred approaches have made little headway in secondary schools generally and it has been left to the de-schooling movement and a few pioneers like A. S. Neill in the private sector of education, to demonstrate what can and cannot be achieved by putting a student's education into his own hands.

As teachers we have a definite and essential role as instructor and inspirer to our students. But Comenius saw the limits of formal instruction three hundred years ago when he wrote of the need 'to seek and find a method by which the teachers teach less and the learners learn more'.

A lack of accommodation, resources or imagination have dis-suaded schools from exploring the promising ideas described in *Images of the Future – A New Approach to the Secondary School*, by Lloyd Trump in 1959.[18] His commission's report envisaged an approach in which 40 per cent of the week might be given to large group instruction, allowing a more generous staffing to be given to 20 per cent of the week for small group discussion and the 40 per cent during which students would work individually.

We must turn again to the whole school. Can we justify our dependence on the class group of thirty as the organisational unit for planning and timetabling? A number of Authorities now use 120 as the organisational group for designing school buildings and a few schools now work and block timetables on that basis. Flexibility in educational building makes easier a flexibility in learning activities. Team teaching is common within some Authority areas but this is normally used to achieve flexibility in student grouping rather than in methods. Consistent block-timetabling could give us more room for manœuvre. Are we being adventurous enough?

Planning the subject content

Whether we start from the student, methods or subject, our planning and consideration of resources must meet the question of subject content. My purpose in this section is not to suggest which topics may be most relevant within a particular subject but to relate fields of knowledge, topics, themes and their development in a way that will assist planning and co-ordination.

Lloyd Trump, the father of team teaching, told American schools in 1966 that they innovated in part and seldom approached their curricular problems as a whole. Does that apply to our secondary schools? Certainly national projects have been undertaken in many sectors of the curriculum but only very recently has any attempt at all been made by the Schools Council to draw threads together. There has been more analysis than synthesis.

The curriculum as a whole is rather indigestible. We need to chart the ground and identify its main areas or fields. I am going to use the term 'field' to indicate an area of knowledge, resources and understanding which represents a corporate, coherent entity and has a body of related concepts. A field may therefore embrace a number of timetabled subjects. Where this occurs, does it not suggest a co-ordinated strategy across subject departments?

Humanities, Man and his Environment, Social Studies and Environmental Studies are examples of accepted but overlapping fields. Since the titles cannot be more specific and because knowledge and concepts can be related in many different patterns, it is unlikely that schools would agree on the subjects covered in each of those fields. It does not matter. No field has an intrinsic validity of content; it represents a wider area of knowledge and resources which is agreed and accepted by a group of teachers as a field of shared and related concepts and concerns. Geography can be seen as a field if the broadest view of it is accepted. Most aspects of Geography however might be accepted within a field of Environmental Studies together with some elements of Science. Alternatively a greater part of Geography might be agreed in a Humanities field involving History, Religious Education, the Arts and some aspects of Language. History, though, could be related to Foreign Languages, Economics and aspects of the Arts in a field of European Studies.

A field of study does not demand integration but it facilitates co-ordination and creates opportunities for interdisciplinary studies. We still tend to regard the curriculum as a collection of subjects. Interests are often divisive. Traditional practice has borne a resemblance to medieval strip farming – it is a pity that the enclosure movement carries such sinister memories. Schools Council projects did not help in this, for those aimed at the young school leaver moved towards a common centre of social relevance so that the same topics and resources were appearing for English, Religious Education, History, Geography and Home Economics without co-ordination.

There is a trend in our newer and larger schools towards wider co-operation and to create senior posts of responsibility over fields [or faculties] rather than subjects: Science, Technology, Creative subjects, Mathematics, Communication, Humanities. In a Nottinghamshire school: departments for Humanities, Creative Design,

Social Studies, Mathematics and Science. In a Northampton school: directors of study in Creative Studies, Social Studies, European Studies, Mathematical Studies and Scientific Studies.

Old wine in new bottles? Or are such fields going to have an integrity and a corporate entity? If the latter, then it will be easier to chart the skills, knowledge, experience and concepts involved and to determine the relationship between courses of study.

A humanities field

If we take the field of Humanities and allow that some aspects of English will fall outside while some elements of Geography go to a related field of scientific studies, the following outline can be suggested:

Field: Humanities (or 'Man and his Environment')

Outline: MAN   – LOOKING AT MAN

                      EXPRESSING HIMSELF

                      CHANGING HIS WORLD

      IN TIME

      AND SPACE

For enquiry work the following 'tool subjects' seem to be involved: Sociology, Anthropology, History, Economics, Archaeology, Geology, Ecology and Political Science. If we wish to ask MACOS-type questions like 'What makes Man human?' and 'How did he become human?', we might add the Science of Animal Behaviour and Psychology.

But enquiry, as we noted earlier, is only one side of the coin. We need to consider the whole aspect of creative experience and imagination, considering the involvement of Drama, Music, Dance, Art and Literature.

The above outline needs to be exploded also in terms of subjects or topics. Among these would be Family, Education, Population, Conservation and Agricultural development. It is not difficult to draw up a comprehensive list. A distinction needs to be drawn between *topics*, which represent factual matter, and *themes*, which are important, recurring ideas or concepts. Examples of specific topics are Family Life in Britain, Australia, Lloyd George, Schools in the nineteenth century; they are areas for enquiry but do not immediately engage creative experience. Examples of themes are

Exploration, Invasion, Survival and Creation; they can draw on a variety of topics and lead readily into creative experience and imagination through Literature, Drama, Music, Art, etc.

Developing a topic or theme

What happens if we take a general topic such as 'Family'. By considering the main ideas and concepts implicit in it we obtain a list of specific sub-topics:

> Topic: *Family*
> function in society
> types of family structure
> roles
> kinship
> genealogy
> marriage and divorce
> socialisation of children
> types of residence
> relations between generations
> relations within generations

Themes, topics and sub-topics can be developed through these eight different dimensions:

> The main ideas or concepts (factual and imaginative).
> The tool subjects (modes of enquiry) involved.
> The opportunities for creative and imaginative experience.
> Location – individual, local, societal, national, global.
> Period – past, present, future.
> Aspects of human behaviour that can arise.
> The controversial issues that may arise.
> Relationships to and within the environment.

Let us take the sub-topic of Family Structures as an example:

> Sub-topic: Types of family structure (age level 15 years).
>   Main ideas and concepts: Extended family, nuclear family.
>   Tool subjects: Sociology, Anthropology, History.
>   Creative and imaginative experience: This is a factual topic, thus Art and Literature are more likely to be used as sources than as media for personal expression.
>   Location: Examples of families in other parts of the world and locally.

Period: Families in the present and the past.
Behaviour: Differences in behaviour (e.g. roles) between family types.
Issues: Is the extended family a better system?
Living with grandma.
Environmental relationship: What factors have caused the breakdown in Britain of the extended family?

It may be helpful to survey likely topics in this way before the starting point and route of a course is chosen. Such a survey also helps co-ordination where more than one department is covering the same topic.

Starting points and routes

If our approach is student-centred to the extent that students direct their own lines of investigation, then it is difficult to anticipate the structure of a course. At present, however, more formal and planned approaches prevail in our secondary schools.

A History specialist is going to be concerned primarily with the dimension of period. He may choose a historical period and relate a number of topics to it, noting the human decisions and events that occurred. He might take a topic such as Medicine to trace its development through historical times.

For a Geography specialist the dimension and whole concept of location may be dominant but with an emphasis on relationships within and between environments. Topics such as commodities and human settlement may be included in a particular course.

A Sociology specialist may relate chosen topics to the local and national situation today, with a sharp eye for the controversial issues that arise.

The specialists in Geography, History and Sociology will each consider the objectives and enquiry methods of their 'disciplines' in building a course and plan to achieve over the longer term a definite pattern, identity and progression. The same concepts can be introduced at higher levels of complexity.

Designing a course in Social Studies, Environmental Studies or Humanities, we would have broader interests and might consider the whole field at the outset. Wishing to involve creative and imaginative work we would prefer themes to topics.

The Humanities team (for such it usually is) are tempted to relate themes to many locations, to the past, present and future, to examine environmental influences and face up to questions of human values. Each of these dimensions could contribute to a wider understanding. Topics concerning Family might be met within each theme. There is a danger of course of skating too lightly over the field and, remembering past pitfalls, particularly at 13–16 age level, the team will judge an insight into human behaviour to be more important than a mere cataloguing of institutions.

The theme or topic as a centre of interest

One way of introducing a theme or topic is to take it as a centre of interest from which the students' lines of enquiry and interest are allowed to radiate, freely or under formal guidance. One difficulty with free student choice is that we cannot easily anticipate the resources needed, nor afford the range that could be demanded. Having identified the possible avenues of enquiry however, we may choose to limit the alternatives in order to provide resources in greater depth. We might even place the alternatives in a sequence to be followed to make organisation easier.

As an example, let us take the lines of study that could stem from a specific topic like 'Our Road':

When was the road built? What is its history?
Who were the men who built the road?
How was the road constructed? What about earlier times?
Why was the road built?
Can we draw and interpret a map of the road?

Our road   Why do different people use the road?
How are people and traffic controlled?
What buildings adjoin and use the road?
How do bridges over it use strong structures?
Has the landscape affected its route?
Has traffic pollution affected near-by vegetation?
Do people like living next to the road?

Such a study could make a great demand on resources but many of them would be found in the local environment. Resource preparation would be much more difficult if we were determined to study roads in general. One of our objectives in using the local environment might be to guide students in framing a suitable way of enquiry.

In History we might take the topic of 'Medieval Life' as the hub.

Though timetabled as History it would surely be interdisciplinary in character:

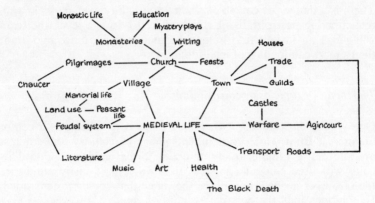

One implication of a diagram like this is that students will not be expected to pursue every line of enquiry but to explore a particular interest or assignment and in doing so to contribute to the whole picture that will emerge. The end of term or half-term exhibition can contribute to this.

A more abstract theme could give more rein to experiential and creative studies in addition to a range of enquiries and analytical studies. This would cater more adequately for what have been called 'the two ways of knowing'. Thus the theme of 'Invasion' suggested these lines to a team of teachers:

Invasion

Invasion of the countryside. Conservation.
How we are invaded and helped by foreign ideas.
Advertisers – are they trying to invade our minds?
Case studies from history of invasion and cultural assimilation.
How people and animals react to invasion.
Studies from literature, including space fiction.
Creative writing.
Art and music work based on the theme.
Drama and dance.

The experience of schools indicates that this imaginative, thematic approach can be more rewarding than more direct topic work because it involves more ways of learning and understanding and is more likely to lead to new insights. For teachers too it can become an exploration. The approach needs careful planning however and the initial inspiration and direction may have to come from the teachers.

The sequential approach

The alternative to the centre of interest and branching topics is a sequence. This imposes an order of succession upon the ideas and sub-topics studied, and is familiar to us through textbooks. Teachers of Mathematics and Foreign Languages argue, with some evidence, that a sequence is required by the nature of learning in their subject. One skill or rule may be essential to the understanding of the next. How often is this essential? The Latin being studied by my daughter begins with these contents:

   I. First conjugation: Present Indicative Active
  II. First declension: Nominative and Accusative cases
 III. First declension: Genitive and Dative cases
 IV. First declension: Ablative case. Prepositions and gender
  V. Second, third and fourth conjugations: Present Indicative Active

It has a familiar ring to me. It seems logical in its order and inhibiting to the use of language, not the manner in which children naturally absorb language when young. Yet resources and bright ideas can put living flesh on even those dry bones.

RESOURCES FOR MOTIVATION

Motivation is of course a constant consideration at all stages of learning and is not seen as an isolated factor. We are considering in this section, however, the initial stimulus and statement with which much work is started. It may be no more than a fleeting introduction to a lesson; it may be a carefully contrived event to launch a term's project. Both will attempt to:

excite the students' interest;
encourage their involvement;
raise questions;
open up suitable areas of study;
make clear the purpose and objective.

Where we as teachers undertake to lead off in a lesson or topic, our choice of resources will be determined by what is available, the nature of the topic and our decision on what is appropriate to the students' age, ability and interests.

A primary head teacher controlling an integrated day approach writes:

'One source for the children was the local craftsmen and other in- habitants. From an old stonemason we borrowed a range of his tools and made an exhibition of them in the school. In this way we could hope to stimulate and provide starting points within the school building for those who came with nothing of their own.'

His last clause is significant for it assumes that many children *will* bring their own ideas and specimens, and indeed in his school the children's own motivation and changing interests are a major driving force. The whole school building is a full, rich, colourful environment – the aestheticism is almost aggressive and the imaginative response from the children often remarkable.

The attractive display of the best primary school environment is not easily emulated throughout the secondary school with its frequent changing of rooms and classes. The dullest and most authoritarian teachers have allowed motivation to be replaced by repression, their bare classroom walls reflecting their lack of resource- fulness. Even the liveliest schools have their occasional deserts but there is a general concern to make our teaching interesting and, to use an over-worn word, relevant. The good English teacher is well versed in the ways of catching his students' imagination and moving them to use language by means of the well-chosen extract, music, a provocative image, a well-read poem. The experienced Drama teacher knows how to fan the embers of enthusiasm into a roaring flame, and the Art teacher how to make the weekly art lesson a feastday.

The above examples involve modes of experience – creative subjects which depend very much on the students' response to stimuli, external and internal, and the material tends naturally to be evocative. What choices are open to the teacher in, say, Mathematics or information subjects? We may explore possibilities for the latter by referring to two topics outlined in the previous chapter.

How may a local road study be launched successfully? An un- adventurous start would be to fall back on teacher-centred ideas – a talk, supported by blackboard work and even a flourish of coloured chalks, or an audio-visual aid with a heavily-overlaid commentary. Easier still, turn to page 11 in the textbook and read about roads '. . . you begin, Brown . . . no, start on line 5. And read that first line again, you missed the full stop! '

We may consider more lively introductions; for example, a visit to the road, or perhaps a visit to the classroom by one of the men working on the road. An exhibition of pictures or roadmen's tools might be used to start off studies, or a good film, television broadcast, record or tape-recording. These depend on resources for the main stimulus and imply prior planning and selection by the teacher or team of teachers involved. How far should planning go? Does the planned topic develop remorselessly through the term, regardless of alternative stimuli that occur? Our subject syllabuses, which generally are still quite strictly adhered to, put a high premium on our ability to inspire and motivate.

We may plan a topic like 'Family' and be prepared for the students' interest to range over many aspects of it without imposing a rigid, sequential order. How might we lead into the topic, noting that the students' experience here can be an advantage? A teacher-centred approach would be to give a lively reading of a suitable poem or book extract, or perhaps to give some personal reminiscences, and go on to elicit students' own experiences. Family snapshots might be used – why after all did astronauts carry their family photos with them to the moon? An exhibition on family life in Victorian times might be available from a local museum service; a film or film extract might be considered or a visitor to talk about his or her family life in a different culture. A current newspaper item or a student's idea might be seized upon by the teacher who has the confidence and knowledge of where resources are available to harness the enthusiasm of the moment.

Consideration might be given to educational games, some of which are designed primarily to give motivation.

Our means of generating interest and involvement in a topic or simply a lesson may merge into the instruction or development that follows. Where we use resources solely for a stimulus, there is no point in continuing beyond the point of impact where a positive response has been achieved. As teachers we become sensitive to this and direct matters accordingly. The final question remains: as to what extent do we accommodate the topics and ideas raised by the students themselves?

RESOURCES FOR INSTRUCTION

Instruction in this context means the transmission to the student and the acquisition by him of a skill, technique or established data.

The wide range of resources available now enables us to assume different roles in the course of instruction. The resources, with their supporting equipment, can sometimes instruct more efficiently than we can.

Teacher-centred

The resource needs for instruction that is still teacher-centred are the professional skills of the teacher and material in a form and medium which leave him dominant. The ability to read and tell a story well has been mentioned, as has the gift of inspiring ideas and commanding respect. The planning of a lesson, in which many of us were instructed in our professional training (presentation, association, application, recapitulation – while moving from the familiar to the new) still holds good.

The teacher's familiar equipment of chalk and blackboard has now been supplemented by the whiteboard. The latter facilitates the use of colour with felt pens and often allows a more imaginative presentation. Its critics complain that the whiteboard is difficult to clean, except with rather obnoxious liquids, and claim that a good rollerboard gives more flexibility. I have found teachers fairly evenly divided on this issue. The overhead projector is a more sophisticated aid but it is easily operated and providing the screen is angled and the transparencies are prepared with care, it is effective. Moreover, a wide range of transparencies may now be obtained commercially which afford a high standard of presentation. Most school projectors of this type are best located in one fixed position but portable models are on the market.

The textbook is of course another traditional instrument of instruction. In its most rigid form it presented a series of lessons which left initiative with the teacher while relieving him of the task of explaining and devising exercises. Resources for teaching – and learning?

This approach, which often assumed that the aim of education was knowledge, was held to be sound and successful in times when authority was less frequently challenged. But apart from our changed social values today, which accord students a greater say in their learning, didacticism has revealed limitations. Class instruction cannot easily reflect the diversity of ideas and ability in even the most carefully streamed class. Because the teacher tends to be more distant from his students, it is more difficult for him to appreciate the needs of particular ages and abilities. Vague terms like 'in ancient times' and 'in the Middle Ages' may cause misunderstanding because the students may be inhibited from asking questions. There is evidence too to indicate that a great many children find difficulty in paying attention to a 'lecture' for more than fifteen or twenty minutes.

The tyranny of the pedant and his blackboard has enriched literature from Dickens' *Dotheboys Hall* to Camara Laye's *African Child*. 'The blackboard was our nightmare. Its dark, blank mirror was the exact reflection of the amount of our knowledge . . . the wretched blackboard magnified every mistake.'[19]

But we should not throw away teacher-centred instruction entirely. It has a place in our armoury.

Reasons for greater use of resources

Three important reasons can be given for the greater use of resources as the agent of instruction: they do not keep the teacher's personality between the student and achievement, and indeed the teacher may not need to be present; secondly, some media can be attractive and highly motivating; thirdly, some materials allow students to proceed at their own pace.

Instructional films, television programmes, filmstrips and slides with tape have proved very successful when used selectively and with a clear purpose. Difficulties have most often been due to lack of preparation, inadequate facilities, poorly maintained equipment and some teacher's lack of expertise in using it. Many schools now have an AVA technician and a well-equipped lecture theatre is no longer a rare facility.

Instruction through audio-visual aids can have an added advantage for less-able students for they need not face a constant succession of reading difficulties. Tape recordings have been found very valuable in meeting such problems in mixed ability groups. As comprehensive schools have adopted mixed ability grouping more widely, the need for such aids has increased.

Programmed learning

'Teach Yourself' books are perhaps more familiar to the adult market than schools but during the 1960s efforts were made to assist self-instruction through programmed learning. This is a means to refine instructional techniques by breaking down learning tasks into their smallest steps and leading the student through them in a logical sequence, checking responses at each step to ensure understanding.

Programmes can be made available when the student requires it or needs it, and he may progress at his individual speed. They may be presented in booklet form, on cards, slides, tape, or on a roll or screen in a teaching machine. Some machines are sophisticated and expensive.

Programmes are classified as linear or branching. The linear moves, as the name implies, in a straightforward sequence of steps. Branching programmes include special routes or diversions to correct misunderstandings revealed by wrong responses or to advance a gifted student.

Considerable claims were made for programmed learning in the late 1960s but this approach has since lost momentum and commercial publishers have been reluctant to invest heavily in it. A number of reasons may be put forward for this: some of the published programmes were of poor quality; programmes were not available for many courses; the cost of the machine-based programmes was high; the time needed to produce a programme seemed out of proportion to the comparatively short period of its use; and after an interval this approach could lack motivation.

Programmed learning has not therefore gained a wide acceptance but the discipline of its analytical study can be a salutary experience for the teacher designing his own materials and it is worthwhile to look more closely at its fundamental form.[20]

In a programme the facts for presentation are divided into the simplest possible steps or frames. These are presented to the student one by one, and after each one a question or task may be set to test comprehension before the student moves on to the next. The correct answers need to be hidden from the student till he has decided on his answer and this can be done simply on a card or booklet by requiring the student to cover the answer column with a piece of card or paper. A programme might there be laid out in this manner:

Frame 1	—
Frame 2	Correct answer to 1
Frame 3	Correct answer to 2
Frame 4	Correct answer to 3
Frame 5	Correct answer to 4

The following examples show how the opening frames might be presented in a programme on volumes.

Here is a bottle of milk
 	
A careless person has knocked it over.
 	
When was there most milk?
    A. When it was in the bottle
    B. After it was knocked over.
    C. The same in both cases.	

First the milk was in the bottle. Then it was spilt over the ground.
    When did the milk cover the most AREA?
        A. On the ground
        B. In the bottle
	C.

AREA and VOLUME do not mean the same thing. One of them describes covering a surface. Which one?
    A. Volume
    B. Area
	A.

	B.

Programming requires a consideration of short objective questions and their form. For example:

1. The capital of Greece is —————.
2. The capital of Greece is — — — — — —.

3. Athens is the capital of Greece. TRUE / FALSE.
4. Philadelphia
   Ithaca
   Athens   is the capital of Greece.
   Rhodes

Each makes different demands upon the student.

Student-centred instruction relies on independent work and may differ by definition from the resources-centred approach only in the degree to which the student is the agent in his learning.

Experiments have been made with 'contracting', by which students contract to undertake certain assignments over a given period. In such a situation a resource centre with extensive independent study facilities would have a major role. A degree of contracting has for many years been one characteristic of Sixth Form studies but plans to make this formally a basis for a whole school have so far enjoyed very limited success.

Feasibility studies are being conducted in computer-assisted learning in which, for instructional purposes, students use computer-controlled teaching machines. By its huge capacity for storage and almost immediate retrieval, the computer can present information to the student on demand, monitor his responses and provide remedial programmes where lack of understanding is revealed. In addition it can keep a full record of each student's progress. Is computer-assisted learning nearer than we think?

Educational games and simulations

Educational games have been introduced into the secondary school a means of giving motivation through participation and competition. We are familiar as parents with snakes and ladders as a useful practice in young children's counting and later the game of Scrabble for spelling. Games have been devised, for example in Mathematics, to encourage students to learn facts or acquire a skill in order to win or reach a target. We might regard such games as educational carrots.

Simulations, which involve students in role play, often without a competitive element, were introduced into this country from America in the 1960s. P. J. Tansey and D. Unwin, in *Simulation and Gaming in Education*,[21] suggest, 'Simulation takes learning out of the area of abstraction and makes it a participatory skill. It involves learning by doing and this is of particular benefit where human reactions, interactions and emotions are involved.'

Geographers will probably know of the American simulation based on the building of the railroads. The students have to know the basic facts before starting and in the course of the simulation they make decisions on the route of their line, see the implications of their decisions and appreciate the hazards faced by the early railroad pioneers.

The Oxfam Committee Game on Botswana requires students to act as a committee and decide on how a limited sum of money should be allocated over a range of projects which are described in detail on information sheets. Again background knowledge must be acquired before the simulation can be undertaken successfully. As part of a fuller study of Botswana the simulation is popular with students, who gain a deeper insight into the real problems of economic development and recognise that there is no single 'correct' answer. A different kind of involvement is gained by Sixth Form students of economics who take part in a Stock Market simulation, which can be highly competitive.

Simulations, it can be claimed, engender a strong motivation and a feeling of relevance. Co-operation rather than competition can be encouraged in processes involving facts, skills and feelings, while a model situation can reduce complexities to an acceptable but none the less realistic level. A few simulations are available from commercial publishers. Simpler simulations such as interviewing can be prepared fairly easily and need few material resources, but more sophisticated exercises need lengthy preparation and initial testing.

Simulations can also play an important role in problem-solving.

Certain questions must remain with us concerning instructional methods. One teacher demonstrating and talking to a large group of, say, 120 students is very economic in terms of resources and staffing. But in what circumstances is this more effective than alternative learning methods? Can we identify the criteria for selecting didactic methods?

Instruction implies conformity, if only in accepting certain structures of knowledge. Where should the balance lie between structure and conformity on one hand and the individual student's style of learning on the other?

RESOURCES FOR SEARCH

Search is used in this context to mean the observing, finding, recording, interpreting and classifying of evidence or data in the manner appropriate to a particular discipline or mode of enquiry. It is the active way of obtaining information and the first phase of enquiry-based learning, or discovery methods, about which so much has been written.

Search cannot be wholly teacher-centred, though the teacher may often plant the evidence. The strategy might be described as surrounding the student with the resources needed for his searches. The teacher enters with his students into a conspiracy to learn.

Two important problems here concern the nature of the resources and the amount of structure and guidance needed to ensure that students' searches are productive. Some teachers argue that the students' enquiries should be disciplined by the recognised rules which, though they are constantly changing at the frontiers of learned research, have proved their worth in a meaningful organisation of knowledge and provided a language by which we can communicate. Others, chiefly in the primary school sector at present, suggest that a student should make his own adjustments to the world he discovers. If we take as an example a child collecting pebbles on a beach. He will tend to organise them and classify them, and the order he selects will have for him a definite validity. There will, however, be many other ways of classifying the pebbles. It may be pointed out that some of these ways have been found to serve useful purposes and are commonly used in order to assist more advanced learning.

The richest and most available resource is the local environment, though this may be more readily seen in schools in pleasant rural surroundings than those in downtown estates. The more child-centred primary schools draw heavily upon their local environment as the field of their children's experience and growth. The stimuli are many, the response often immediate and natural. Children can surely only make valid judgements within the limits of their own experience.

I have an idea that the ideal education begins, in childhood, in the depths of the countryside and moves gradually towards the urban situation, perhaps reaching Piccadilly Circus, with critical awareness well-developed, at the age of eighteen. With increasing maturity the student can handle vicarious evidence and his horizons will expand far beyond those of his neighbourhood, but the value of 'real' resources cannot be ignored.

The environment yields itself, leaving the searcher to impose a structure, raise related ideas into concepts, organise the data into subjects and to respond from the imagination. It is the source of those raw materials such as stone, clay and wood, the exploration of which leads to the learning of manipulative skills and the time-honoured traditions of the craftsmen. These world materials are also a medium of expression by which the student shapes and gives tangible form to his inner state and feelings. This searching is the mode of experience.

A significant trend in education over the last two decades has been the wider use of original material in preference to the predigested information upon which the author or teacher has already imposed an interpretation. Historians now place more emphasis on archives, visits and well-supervised 'digs', and a number of Local Authorities have museum services for schools. But what if Africa is the subject of study? One suspects that few, if any, of those well-known textbook authors ever visited the continent. Their material was superficial, sometimes inaccurate and soon out-of-date. Why not let the Africans speak for themselves – either in person or through indigenous materials?

Another recent trend has been towards a greater diversity of learning material, stemming both from interdisciplinary courses and more imaginative schemes within specialist subjects. A study of the seventeenth century now will often embrace not only the historical events but the diaries, art, crafts and music of the time. Films, slides, reference books, actual objects and records have become acceptable sources for search.

One result of more active learning methods and the use of themes has been the disappearance in some subjects of the traditional lesson format. Instead of the short, complete entity, a variety of methods may extend the study of a theme over a half or full term. Resources may therefore be required for a long period.

The further a topic is from students' direct experience, the greater the need for us to assemble and arrange evidence. Take, for example, a study of the Australian Aborigines – looking at survival in a society with a limited technology. Being aware that few suitable reference books are available at the level we have in mind, we may decide to prepare ourselves a booklet of information on the Aborigines. Access to anthropological literature would give us more original sources. Should we organise the material under headings which an anthropologist would use?

To what extent should our resources direct our students' study and responses? Surely we would indicate the Dewey classification that would enable students quickly to refer to relevant books in the school and public library. But should our information be in a stapled booklet which has a sequential order and is easy to handle and store, or in looseleaf, non-book form that allows greater freedom in use? Should studies be undertaken individually or in small groups, and if the latter how should the groups be formed?

Some of the most successful work now being done in schools uses a study guide separate from the evidence or reference material. This has flexibility. Thus a study guide might assist and raise questions in our student's study of the Aborigines' encouraging them to think like an anthropologist and at the same time to organise their own feelings and reactions. Their searches might in this case lead them to:

> reference books
> the prepared booklet of information
> tapes of music, legends, and information
> GUIDE sets of slides in wallets with notes and small group viewers
> pictures and wall charts
> exhibits
> fiction

Some of these resources might be linked. For example, a tape might describe and raise questions on pictures or the slides, or present readings of the legends and fiction for poor readers.

One group of teachers from several schools co-operating to design materials on the Aborigines for 11–13-year-old children approached the problem in this way and started the term's study guide on these lines:

STUDY GUIDE

A person who is qualified to study groups of primitive people and their way of life is called an ANTHROPOLOGIST. His subject is called ANTHROPOLOGY.

Our visitor was an anthropologist. What did he tell us? He said that he could not collect new facts from books. He had to go to live among the people he studied in order to observe their way of life. He had to learn their language so that he could talk with them. Only in this way could he understand their ideas and beliefs.

An anthropologist collects his evidence carefully. He makes notes under particular headings. He is interested in these things: APPEARANCE, ECONOMY (ways of getting wealth and food), TOOLS and WEAPONS, SHELTER (homes), FAMILY AND OTHER GROUPS (social organisation), LEADERSHIP AND THE WAY THEY RULE THEMSELVES (political organisation), RELIGION (beliefs and customs), LANGUAGE, ART, MUSIC.

THINKING ABOUT IT

The ideas of the Aborigines may seem strange to us. Their old way of life can be called 'primitive'. By this we mean that their tools and weapons were very simple and their language could not be written. Later on you will have to think carefully about what 'primitive' means.

Do not think that all Aborigines today live the kind of life you are going to study. Some live a modern way of life in Australian cities. Remember Yvonne Goolagong, the famous tennis player? But a few keep to the old ways.

We must seem strange to other people. Just imagine a visitor coming from another planet to observe us. He might report something like this:

'These beings are certainly peculiar. Soon after darkness comes they go to special places in their shelters and there they put on a different covering. Then they put themselves on a low platform, covered with fabrics made from plants and animal furs, and lose consciousness until light returns. They seem to fear the dark.'

What is he looking at?

Imagine you are a visitor from outer space. Write down your observations on seeing one of these:

A football match. A birthday party. Your street.

Now begin your study.

Use the books and other aids which are available. These are listed at the back of this guide. Books on anthropology in you local library will be found on shelf section 572.

Here are some questions to help you in your study. Ask your teacher for help when you need it. Make rough notes first and finish these before you start on your own report.

This guide also gives you some questions to think about deeply. You may discuss these in small groups. You may have questions of your own to talk about too. But first the search:

THE ABORIGINES OF AUSTRALIA

What do they look like?

Are they tall or short?

What colour is their hair and skin?

How would you describe their faces?

Can you draw an aborigine?

What clothing do they wear? What is it made of?

Why do they wear the clothing they do?

Other groups have chosen to divide the term's study into half a dozen units which look in turn at the surroundings, family life, economy, religion and myths, arts and current predicament of the Aborigines. Each unit has a short study guide and also a filesheet which the student works upon and puts into his file alongside his individual work. One study guide looks like this:

STUDY GUIDE: THE ABORIGINES AND THEIR SURROUNDINGS

Read the booklet and other aids to help you on this topic.

FILESHEET — Work on the filesheet for this topic. It includes studies with maps. Put the filesheet into your file when you have completed it.

READING — Start reading in your spare time 'The Rocks of Honey' by Patricia Wrighton.

DISCUSSION — Here are some questions for you to talk about in your working groups. The space is for your own questions:

Whereabouts in Australia today are Aborigines still leading their old way of life? Why are they only in those areas?

If you crash-landed in a plane 500 miles west of Alice Springs, having only what you have with you now, what would you do?

What skills did the Aborigines use in order to survive in the Australian bush?

What causes the desert in Australia?

PRACTICAL — Draw a rainfall and temperature graph for Alice Springs, using the figures in the booklet.

You could prepare an illustrated guide to the wild animals of the Australian 'bush' or design a poster showing a 'bush' scene for the tourist trade.

WRITING — What was your reaction to the film showing the Aborigines and their surroundings? Can you describe your feelings?

These study guides apply the information gathered by searching to the consideration of problems as a natural extension of study.

Enquiry need not be a protracted method. Nuffield Science schemes sometimes used an exhibition of materials within the laboratory to gain an objective over a double period. Visits may be made to environmental sites and museums. A local street may be the basis of a short environmental study. Experience shows the value of thorough preparation for visits and of notes or study sheets which lead the students' attention to the main items of interest. Some museums provide notes, questionnaires and speakers by arrangement. The service offered by the Commonwealth Institute in London is exemplary.

A flexible organisation within the classroom is important to enquiry methods. I will leave to a later chapter the faculty resource centre and consider the classroom as a virtually self-contained entity. The grouping of students which arises naturally from search methods is markedly different from those dictated by most instructional methods. These diagrams illustrate the contrast.

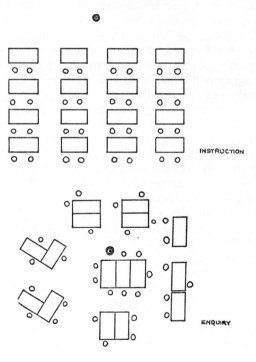

Where the more active learning methods are used constantly, grouping cannot be static for students will need to move to the resources and equipment they require. Organisation is then made easier if the room is planned on the basis of activities. The diagram below is an example:

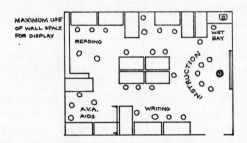

Let us take a classroom where the Aborigine material is being used and freeze the activity briefly. What is going on?

Four students are sitting in the book corner and one is making notes for the group. A further two students are reading fiction. Three more are writing at a near-by table.

In another corner four students, also working as a group, are listening with headsets to a cassette recording of a traveller's impressions. A recording of music for the 'corroboree' is also available. Two girls are using a small projector in a dark corner to view a black and white filmstrip on Aborigine life.

Several are working on maps and one boy is making a graph from rainfall figures. In the corner near the sink, four students are busy together on a large painting of an Australian scene while two others are painting, one copying Aborigine patterns and the other illustrating a story from the 'Dreamtime'. The latter subject furnished ideas for an earlier class dramatisation of legends and one girl is still writing a poem that arose out of this.

Some students are therefore searching, others are responding to ideas. Two groups are discussing questions and applying their evidence and feelings. The teacher is with one of these groups, which is talking about the plight of Aborigines in Australian cities. The other group, having discussed the problem of surviving immediately after a plane crash in the desert, are wondering what they would do if they met a group of Aborigines. 'And what,' one girl is saying, 'will they think of us?'

Work stemming from search alone is often descriptive but lacking in intellectual demand. The following questions might therefore be asked both by the teacher in planning studies and the student starting his enquiry:

Exactly what is to be found out?
What kind of questions need to be asked?
What subject or kind of enquiry is involved?
What person has expert knowledge on these matters?
Where can evidence or data be found?
How can it be observed?
How can it best be recorded?
Under what headings should information be collected?
Is the information relevant?
Is it original?
Does the evidence need interpretation?
Is the source reliable?
Is it fact, opinion or fiction?
Is it up-to-date?
Can different sources be compared?
Should sources be recorded?
Should a bibliography be included?

This sharpening of search methods is not the whole matter. In his exploration the student will relate findings to his individual experience and emotions. By finding out about the world around him and learning how to learn, the student learns a little more about himself, his identity and relationships. The affective side of enquiry is difficult to appraise, and the most common argument for these more active methods is that in a world where change is constant and knowledge is exploding it is vital that students should first know how to find out the information they need. A still stronger argument might be seen in the idea that this is one of the natural ways in which we learn and grow.

RESOURCES FOR PROBLEM-SOLVING

Knowledge should be put to work – not just recorded in flowery folders and the museums of the mind. Application was uppermost in Mr Squeers' thoughts when, after the spelling of 'winders', he set boys to clean them. Our purpose however will be to encourage students in proposing solutions to problems, making and justifying decisions.

We do not yet fully understand how students learn to reason.

Evidence suggests that some proceed naturally by trial and error, some by sudden insight and others by models or gradual analysis. Formal procedures move from the search for information to the forming of a hypothesis and the testing of it.

We may usefully distinguish at this point between the various situations in which problems arise. A controversial issue may lead to heated discussion and the formulation of opinions which must be justified by reference to the evidence available. Solutions here are likely to be value judgements. A factual problem on the other hand can have one correct solution and ideas can be tested against established facts. A brief practical challenge can arise in many subjects, while a significant development among the craft subjects has been the introduction of project technology courses in which both boys and girls may select a problem, find out the facts, draw up a design for a solution, build it and test it. The problem could be to build a small hovercraft or a better chair for classroom use. It has been said that project technology is more a method than a subject. Even in modes of experience such as dance and painting, knowledge and techniques may be applied with feeling and imagination to a new challenge in order to work out a satisfying solution.

The contribution of disciplines to questions and wider issues, which may be life-like and life-size, is the real ground of integration or inter-disciplinary courses.

How far can problem-solving be a teacher-centred activity with the resources mainly in the teacher's hands? There is perhaps the temptation in elaborating the problem to give the answer too or to act like the science teacher who told his class half-way through a 'Nuffield' problem. 'I've marked your predictions. Now go ahead and see what happens'. A gifted teacher can tease the solution step by step from his class, taking a short cut to understanding, but many individuals will have little opportunity to participate actively or put forward and test their own ideas. So often in the past, application of knowledge has taken the form of teachers directing their students to an exercise in the textbook.

How to set about a problem is itself a problem of methodology. The following questions may be adapted to help both teacher and student in a project-type problem:

Before starting
  Is the problem clear and easy to understand?
  Are the necessary facts and materials available?
  Where can the facts be found?
  How can they be obtained?

Considering the evidence
    Is the information up-to-date?
    Are the statements fact, fiction or opinion?
    Should different sources be checked?
    What is the balance of evidence?

Considering the conclusion
    What conclusion or hypothesis can be made?
    What qualifications need to be made?
    What are the implications?

Presenting and testing the conclusion
    How can the solution be made or presented?
    How can it be tested?
    How can it be justified?

The point must be stressed that problem-solving activities for younger students should be 'concrete' in nature for they generally find great hardship in abstractions.

We can illustrate the various methods appropriate to the consideration of problems by taking again the topic of the local road, assuming that changes are being made which arouse social controversy.

Simulation: An actual local situation or a model might be taken where alternative plans exist for building a by-pass or widening a main road. Students could be encouraged to take the role of residents with vested interests and authorities with expert evidence and to prepare their arguments for a forthcoming public enquiry when a community decision should be reached. A major aim in this would be to give a deeper understanding of interactions in decision-making in communities. Resources for this would include maps and information.

Alternative simulations could represent an Authority's Highways Committee deciding on a road scheme, given census and development figures and local opinion. A Housing Committee might consider conflicting applications for the future of a terrace house occupied by an elderly couple but on a convenient line for road realignment. If housing is a topic for study, the game prepared by 'Shelter' might be considered.

Game: Educational games include a competitive element, which may not be considered desirable and appropriate to many situations. A game might however be devised on building a new road or motorway given certain criteria and information. The transportation of goods might also prove a rewarding subject.

Discussion: Discussion is talking with others. It is in fact a sophisticated activity. Henry Miller said, 'When one really begins to talk one delivers himself'. Do we often attain that level in school? Or is most discussion just disguised instruction dominated by ourselves as teachers?

The Schools Council Humanities Project directed by Lawrence Stenhouse was the first attempt to develop discussion methods in depth, stating at the beginning of its Introduction that 'the mode of enquiry should have discussion, rather than instruction, as its core', and that 'discussion should protect the divergence of view among participants rather than attempt to achieve consensus'. These suggestions, of course, referred to the discussion of controversial issues. The Project's approach places the teacher in a neutral, non-authoritarian role and provides banks of loose-leaf material representing a balanced range of evidence, to which teacher and students should have immediate access. Each published unit contains several hundred items and the unit on 'Living in Cities' would have material relevant to studies of roads with the 14+ age range. Book and film lists are included for the teacher, who is encouraged to add further material, particularly items of local interest.

The unpredictability of good discussion demands flexibility in resource materials, and where reference to a bank of information is considered essential, much expense can be incurred. An efficient system of retrieving such material is also required.

Where discussion is geared mainly to the interpretation and re-ordering of personal experience, less support is needed from material resources. A photograph, cartoon or short story may be a sufficient catalyst. The 'Lifelines' material published by the Schools Council Moral Education project relies on quite short texts, situations and drawings to spark off discussion with limited guidance.

Discussion involving objective or 'scientific' learning will tend to be convergent and the teacher may guide it towards the one solution that is acceptable. But where controversial issues and value judgements are concerned, resources may be disqualified by the teacher who uses the discussion to assert his own views or gives praise to individuals for their particular point of view rather than for their quality of expression.

We should introduce or encourage discussion for a purpose, not for its own sake. The actual route for a new road might be considered more objectively, and perhaps with expert assistance, in discussion as opposed to the simulated role play situation already described. Discussion might centre on such now controversial issues as the right of people to drive their cars and motorcycles into city centres when they wish to. Indeed, with the world's limited resources of oil, is it worth building any more roads?

Some attempts have been made to design resources for discussion in order to lead students through a logical succession of steps on a given problem. A short booklet may be programmed so that students discuss a set range of carefully prepared questions, state their conclusions, and are then faced with the implications of their conclusions. The value of training on these more structured lines must be weighed against the possibility of reduced motivation and the inhibition of individual ideas not anticipated in the structure.

Case Study: The case-study method invites a greater involvement in discussion by identification with the situation or characters portrayed in the case study. The resources required here are copies of a report (*c.* 400–800 words) describing a case, person or situation in simple terms, with quotations or even in the first person, and without any judgement upon it. The case study could be tape-recorded. Experience shows that young people quickly identify sufficiently with people in a relevant case study to be able to discuss it. They move from the objective case to introduce their personal experience in a way that they would seldom do if prompted directly. As Pauline and George Perry point out in their *Case Studies in Adolescence,*[22] students recognise that their own problems are shared by many other people and they come to understand other people a little better and appreciate the reasons for their behaviour.

The essence of the case-study method is identification and involvement, and these are most easily found in topics related to our students' family life, employment prospects, relations with the opposite sex, etc. The road study does not appear to be a very fertile one in this respect, but the case of a single person or family in a threatened house or a fatality on a busy stretch of road might be considered.

A problem of a very different nature would be to discover why particular types of stone are used for the foundations, surface and kerbs of roads. Younger students would need at least to obtain certain instruments and to learn about the Moh scale. But is it a problem worth setting if students do not raise it themselves? It depends on the weighting you give to thinking methods as opposed to content. Some middle school teachers, for example, might argue in the words of the popular song, 'It's not what you do, it's the way that you do it'.

A more demanding exercise, interdisciplinary in context, would be the design of a new council estate and its homes. Decisions could hardly in this case be carried forward into commitment, but models could be constructed and the local Authority's departments for Architects and Housing might be counted among the resources available, and perhaps also the Social Services. This indeed is an example of a problem that can become the topic. I see no reason why students should not be involved in the planning of new extensions to their school.

The resources needed for the more active learning methods of finding, evaluating and applying information are more numerous than those required for many instructional methods because the resources are put in the students' hands rather than the teacher's. As individual and small group activity is extended, the need grows for audio-visual equipment designed for this purpose, for example: cheap individual filmstrip and slide viewers, made of plastic and using natural light; battery-powered small group viewers; mains-powered small projectors and screens; small tape-recorders or cassette players (assuming that recorders are also available in the school) with a junction box allowing six headsets to be plugged in, avoiding noise and disturbance in the learning area.

Topics and problems which are divergent rather than convergent in nature also raises the demand for material resources.

These demands soon reach a level where schools begin to question the economics and existing management techniques in a developing educational approach which they hold to be educationally sound. We shall consider the management of resources. The main questions remaining from this chapter concern the type and degree of structure that is desirable in our resources and the extent to which the individual student may direct his own course of study.

RESOURCES FOR PRESENTATION

When students prepare to present their ideas and findings in a finished form, the demand for resources changes significantly. Audio-visual equipment may now be seen as creative tools instead of as media for conveying knowledge for learning. Aids go into reverse: the camera which first provided slides and photograph for study now works in the students' hands to capture in visual form their own work and discoveries; the tape-recorder used to provide information and motivation may now be used by students to record and present their responses; the videotape-recorder which recorded off-air and made available the televised programme may, with camera, be the means by which students give their own interpretation. These are some of the possibilities. Even the blackboard can be taken over by the students.

Presenting their work, our students are no longer interested in resources already prepared and digested. They want raw material and tools: paper, card, pen, paintbrush, paint, tape, film, glue, scissors, crayon. With these they can fashion their own resources, express their ideas and establish their own identities.

What secondary schools so often lack in these circumstances is space. The size of traditional classrooms, the narrowness of corridors, and the constant succession of classes through specialist rooms all dictate again the building of displays and exhibitions which add prestige to study and help to draw together ideas around important concepts. In fact, secondary schools have about 50 per cent more area per pupil than primary schools, but they have locked it up in a variety of specialist facilities and insisted that some of these must stand idle at any given time if a timetable is to be feasible.

Schools with determination can overcome many of these difficulties and transform their internal, and often their external, environment. Much of the finest work I have seen in secondary schools has been in poor accommodation. I must say however that few of our secondary schools have been designed with any consideration for imaginative display.

I heard a teacher recently say of formal teaching methods, 'we give so much – and we get back so little'. Is the students' response not a fair reflection of the relevance and quality of what we put into the teaching situation? Are we really harnessing the energies of our students?

We may set out as richly laden with resources as 'quinquireme of Nineveh from distant Ophir', but unless we are confident of sailing in the right direction and win an equally resourceful response from those upon whom we bestow our wares, we may have laboured in vain.

Chapter 3

Practical Problems

DESIGNING RESOURCES

Methods help to shape the resources we select or design. Where we intend to encourage divergent thinking rather than convergent, and where we aim to promote individualised learning, our resources are more likely to be non-sequential in structure and more flexible. In these circumstances looseleaf sheets will have advantages over the bound book and a set of slides will be preferred to a filmstrip.

Teachers designing resources in schools tend to concentrate on non-sequential or more flexible materials. There are several reasons for this: materials are often needed to support new courses and methods for which commercial publishers have made inadequate provision, whereas the teacher content to rely on textbooks is relatively well served; flexible material, in smaller units, take less time, money and expertise to produce physically and lends itself more easily to that constant revision which is the price of progress.

We have already noted the deeper understanding of methods and the use of materials that can be instilled by practical involvement. We must now balance that advantage against the mediocrity that can result in a school where the processes are not clearly understood: the sea of poorly typed, hastily reproduced worksheets; the flimsily fabricated Humanities course which is a joy only to its creators. The publisher's textbook may be sequential and leave no surprises for the coming months, but it is now more likely to be stimulating and attractive in format, leaving ends open.

There is a significant difference between the design of resources that is a reaction against formal methods and that which is action to achieve clearly defined objectives.

It is often stated that schools can produce material more cheaply than the commercial publishers. It is true that we buy much in a textbook or kit which we do not require, but if we cost not only the raw material but also the time taken by professional and ancillary staff to produce our finished items, we may find in most cases that we are paying considerably more. School-made resources carry hidden costs which are often represented by our leisure time. We may be willing to give that time and accept a lack of professional finish in order to produce resources which meet more effectively our specific objectives. There is some evidence that intense effort of this kind cannot be sustained for more than three years. Difficulties could be alleviated if teacher-release were more common and if block time-tabling were introduced with built-in time for team planning.

Let us now consider the important questions concerning the design of a resource item:

Who is going to handle it – teacher or student?

Is the idea being pitched at the right student level?

Is the most effective method being employed? Take, for example, the topic of authority and abuse of power. We might consider Hitler as a case study, look at a film on baboons, look at an 8mm film of a playground at breaktime, observe young chicks, introduce a role play situation, or dramatise a historical incident. Have we considered sufficient alternatives?

Is original material, or the real thing, available?

Which medium meets the particular need? A tape, for example, can carry music and original voices, and it can transmit one teacher's excellent voice to more students.

Is the vocabulary at the right ability level?

Are the sentence structures too complex?

Is additional material needed for the most or least able?

Are we asking the right questions? Are we allowing the students to ask their own questions?

Should questions and problems be separate from the material to be studied?

What size should be adopted for paper? Many schools have now adopted A4 as a standard size, though in 1973 one national education centre was still handing visitors three different sizes. A5 (210 × 150 mm), which is A4 folded across its length, is more convenient for handling. Some schools have retained 9″ × 7″ because it fits their existing exercise books.

Are there advantages in using coloured paper? If so, should colours be used in a consistent way, for example to indicate types of material or ability levels? Is the school consistent in any such policy?

Is colour duplication needed for type and diagrams? Will spirit duplication meet the need? Is the use of colour drums on ink duplicators worth the extra labour?

Is the page well laid out? Is there too much text on the page? Are there generous margins? Is the 'justifying' of typed lines (making them end on the same vertical line) worth the extra time it takes?

Is the title eye-catching? Is it worthwhile using 'Letraset' or an equivalent type of stencilled lettering?
Is the typeface suitable? Does an electric typewriter with carbon ribbon earn its keep?

`This was a typewriter with proportional spacing.`

`This was a typewriter with ordinary spacing.`

This was a 'jumbo' typewriter.

The design of resources must anticipate the limits and advantages of the processes available to reproduce them. Where multiple copies are going to be required, we need either to make a stencil by hand or prepare a master copy from which a stencil or photocopies can be made. The nature of the original will determine the process that can be employed.

The main processes are outlined below:[23]

Spirit duplication

Method: A spirit-master stencil can be made from a master copy (which should not include tone pictures) by use of a thermographic copier, but it is far better to produce your original on a spirit stencil sheet, using the colour carbon sheets as required. In either case copies are run off on a spirit duplicator.

Advantages:
  A quick and fairly cheap process.
  Use of colour.

Disadvantages:
  Image deteriorates through duplication.
  Maximum run may be 100 in some cases.
  Copies fade with exposure to light.
  Freshly duplicated copies smell of spirit.

Quality of copies: Poor to fair.

Thermographic stencil

Method: The original, which must have a mineral base (so typing is best done with a carbon ribbon attachment and lines in pencil or indian ink) and which should not include tone pictures, is passed through a thermographic copier with a special stencil. This heat-transfer process gives a stencil which can be put on an ink duplicating machine.

Advantages:
    Quick and fairly cheap.
    Maximum run 500+ and copies are durable.

Disadvantages:
    Image deteriorates.
    Stencil is difficult to store and use again (in fact it is better to make another stencil).

Quality of copies:
    Poor to satisfactory.

Electronic scanner stencil

Method: Original, which may include tone pictures and colour (reproduced in tones of black), is put on to an electronic scanner machine alongside a special stencil. The finished stencil is used on an ink duplicator.

Advantages:
    Tone picture can be reproduced (and e.g. photocopied archives).
    Maximum 500+ and copies are durable.
    Stencil can be stored and gives good results.

Disadvantages:
    Electronic scanning machine is expensive (*c.* £500).
    Stencils take 5–15 minutes to make.
    Ink duplicator needs silk screen instead of standard cloth screen to give best results.

Quality:
    Fair to good.

Ink duplication

Method: Original material must be typed on to an ordinary duplicating stencil and line work added with a stylus. The stencil is used on an ink duplicator, which can add a second colour on a second run if a different ink drum is available.

Advantages:
  Cheap and quick.
  Stencil can be stored. Maximum run is 500+ and copies are
    durable.

Disadvantages:
  Typing with a shaded typeface gives poor results.
  Stylus-drawn lines are not crisp.

Quality of copies:
  Fair to satisfactory.

Off-set litho

Method: Original may be transferred on to an off-set litho stencil/
plate by using one of several machines. Alternatively, typing and
line drawings may be put directly on to a cheaper off-set litho stencil.
In either case the stencil/plate is used on an off-set litho printing
machine.

Advantages:
  Paper is pleasant to feel and see.
  Students can easily write on off-set paper.
  Running costs can be cheaper than duplication.
  Good quality reproduction.

Disadvantages:
  High capital outlay to establish system.
  Full-time operator is needed, to make it economic, though table-
  top machines are now automated to the extent that operation is a
  simple matter.
  Photographs need a very expensive, professionally made plate to
  give really good results.

  Quality of copies:
  Satisfactory to very good.

Copier

Method: Original is fed through either a thermographic (heat-
transfer) copier, which gives quick, cheap but poor quality copies
from images with a mineral base only; a flat-bed copier which takes
more time and expense to produce better quality copies from any
images; a chemical-developer copier which will produce better copies
of illustrations; or an electrostatic machine which is much more expensive and much more efficient. Photocopying is not economic un-

less, say, five or less copies are needed for a limited period of time.

The do-it-yourself movement in schools has created a demand for a reprographic unit as part of schools' centralised facilities. Can we afford the facilities and machines? What scale of ancillary help is implied? Are we confident of the cost–effectiveness? Should we look to agencies such as teachers' centres for certain facilities?

CLASSIFYING AND INDEXING FOR RETRIEVAL

'Lord, help me to keep what I find
And to find what I keep.'

It might be any resource-minded teacher's prayer. As more active learning methods have created the need for a greater range of resources to be held, management problems have increased. This has led to the school resource centre movement.

The first criterion in selecting a system for organising resources is that it should allow students and teachers to obtain what they want as easily and as quickly as possible. A system will involve classifying materials and indexing them for retrieval. The methods of doing this have frequently aroused a passion that was reserved eight years ago for the discussion of mixed ability grouping. Let us therefore try to examine the issues objectively.

Classification

How should knowledge be inter-related?
In what kind of order should we store and display our materials?
It is one of the first problems faced by librarians. The two real alternatives are by subject/topic or by accession number. Shelving items by accession number may be economic of space and a librarian's time, but it is not helpful to the teacher or student looking for material on a given topic. In the school library, where students will browse as well as search for specific items, there seems no justification for a shelf order dictated by other than subject/topic. Arguments may however be made for using accession number order for certain non-book materials such as slide sets, tapes and records, especially if they are being stored for limited access. The number of such items in a secondary school may be relatively small and there are considerable difficulties involved in placing them on or near shelves with books on the same topic. Accession numbers are certainly a valuable device for relating printed items to their original copies and stencils.

Of the library systems used for subject classification,[24] by far the most common is that originally developed by Dewey in America at the end of the last century. Under constant revision, it is based on a decimal order with books grouped in subjects in a sequence up to 999. Figures added after the decimal point can give a very precise location, though some common contemporary topics have rather obscure numbers. This classification embraces all subjects. It has the merit of bringing many related subjects together but it does not do so consistently enough for some teachers. For example, material on Australian Travel and Geography will be located at 919·4; on Australian History at 994; on Aborigines at 572·899* and Aboriginal Music at 784·7. This is fine for the specialist but less helpful if we wish to pursue an interdisciplinary study. The Dewey classification is nevertheless a proven system based on many years' experience and students will almost certainly meet it in visiting public libraries. A qualified librarian or experienced assistant is needed to run it very efficiently.

Some teachers have defined the limits of their needs and attempted to devise a subject classification which is better adjusted to educational practice. Within a classroom or departmental resource area this can have advantages but, as Norman Beswick suggests in Schools Council Working Paper 43,[25] ambitious attempts meet the same problems as Dewey and the results are often much worse. Can we really justify a system that is unique to the central organisation of one school?

There are other schemes of subject classification but space does not permit their description here.

We also need to classify resources according to media or type. This will determine the sort of storage needed. Identifying the medium can therefore direct us to the appropriate location. There are obvious merits in adopting a list of media designations that is common to all schools and agencies. The following list includes most of the types normally found in schools:

Cutting (extract from printed publication)	Microfiche (miniature on flat sheet of film)
Film	Microscope slide
Filmstrip	Model
Folder	Negative
Globe	Overhead transparency
Kit (multi-media)	Pamphlet
Loop (film loop)	Person (as a source)
Map	Photograph

* 'Primitive peoples' may now be classed under 301·2.

Picture	Tape (on spool)
Place	Tape cassette
Realia	Videotape (spool)
Record	Videotape cassette
Single sheet	Wall chart
Slide	

Indexing

Indexing should make the best of subject classification, iron out the problems arising, point to resources, sources and information available elsewhere, indicate relationships between materials which are particularly relevant to the student or teacher, and of course facilitate retrieval.

We must consider indexing in relation to the questions we naturally ask when searching for resources. We may first enquire about the availability of:

Material on a particular subject.

Material by a particular author or producer.

A specific item.

In the first two our request may also cover sources and information.

Having found out what is available, noting the media involved, we go on to question the specification of the items (for example, for a filmstrip – the content and number of frames, size of frames, colour or black and white), author, the suggested interest/ability range, date of issue, the time and place of its subject content, and, most important, where it can be obtained. We normally need to know these things before we select the material suited to our purpose.

A five-by-three inch (or metric equivalent) library card might be made out on this pattern:

MEDIA DESIGNATION		DEWEY CLASSIFICATION
AUTHOR/PRODUCER		
TITLE		
PUBLISHER	DATE	
SPECIFICATION & SYNOPSIS		
SUGGESTED AGE RANGE AND INTEREST RANGE		
LOCATION		
ACCESSION NUMBER		SUBJECT(S)

This card would tell us what we want to know about a particular item and it is laid out for inclusion in a classified catalogue – that is, a catalogue in which the cards are put in Dewey decimal order. This would be supported by an author catalogue in alphabetical order. This is the system found in most public libraries and it represents an existing national pattern which can be extended to cover non-book material. One disadvantage claimed by some is that we must refer to a card catalogue or booklet first to find the Dewey decimal classification if we do not know it.

The information on the index card may be rearranged slightly so that it can put into a dictionary catalogue, which sets out its cards for author/producer and title/subject in one joint alphabetical order. This has some advantages but it does not bring together related topics. An alternative to the dictionary catalogue is the alphabetical catalogue which has separate alphabetical orders for subjects and authors, but this again does not group related topics.

In any of these catalogues multiple card entries may be made to give cross references where an item is relevant to more than one topic. This frequently arises, for example, with visual aids.

Co-ordinate indexing, the main alternative to the card subject index, is based on accession numbers for retrieval. It uses a feature list sheet for giving the full information we require about an item. Each item has a feature list which is stored in accession number order, as are the items.

The best-known of the co-ordinate indexing systems in schools is that often referred to as occi, the optical-coincidence index. A feature list is made out for each item, which is given an accession number. The number is then punched out on one or more feature cards or sheets which contain 5,000 or 10,000 minute numbered squares. There is a feature card for each topic to be covered. Thus a new item on CANALS is given its accession number, say 4561, and the feature card for CANALS has a hole punched at square 4561. The light showing through this hole when the card is held up to light indicates the accession number of an available item. If the item is also relevant to Lancashire and the eighteenth century, then the feature cards for these topics may also be punched at 4561. If these three cards are held up together, light appears at 4561, a planned optical coincidence. In this way cross-referencing can be extended to a considerable degree (though problems can arise with books because items from different contexts may be related) and this is held to be one of the chief assets of the system. It is more difficult to discard items in this type of indexing, and two operations are required to give the information required about an item. Schools using it however often find it attractive to use. It has been in service in schools only for a few years and evaluation would be premature. In 1973 almost all the schools using the optical coincidence system were operating it separately from the school library and chiefly for non-book materials. Can this be justified? Or is it wiser to develop and extend our existing libraries to cope with non-book material?

Another form of co-ordinate indexing uses 'Uniterm cards' and this system is used in a few schools. There is a card for each topic covered and accession numbers of items are entered on appropriate cards in a column from 0–9 according to the last digit of the accession number. This is a simple but fairly effective way of cross-referencing for it is easier to see whether the same item appears on two or more topic cards. Clearly it has limits.

Is one system of indexing for retrieval superior to the others for secondary school needs in organising resources more centrally? In the Schools Council Working Paper 43, the Resource Centre project deliberately sat on the fence. A further paper, reporting on the experiences of six pilot schools, has not been published at the time of writing. It was unfortunate that the six schools did not cover a representative range of systems, I would suggest the following criteria be considered:

It should not divide books from non-book material but show the availability of both in one system.
It should be efficient and not difficult to operate.
It should make teachers and students aware of related topics.
It should facilitate the degree of cross-indexing which is genuinely required.
It should show sources, ideas, information, people and places which are readily available to the school and educationally helpful.
It should not isolate the school as a system but should be part of a network with certain standardised procedures so that wider communication is encouraged, materials may be easily exchanged, and links established with area or regional agencies loaning and giving material to the school. Such a service is likely to be based on five-by-three inch cards for these can be printed and sent with material from, say, a regional centre.

Different criteria apply where only a departmental or faculty resource organisation is being considered.

One future development of which we must be aware is computer retrieval. Automatic systems are already used in industry to retrieve information. Computer assistance may first be available at national level for the cataloguing of non-book materials and feasibility studies are already being undertaken by several bodies, including the Council for Educational Technology. One further criterion for our system should therefore be that it is suited for transfer to computer tape or punched cards and for receiving information back from a regional or national system.

ACCESS, STORAGE AND REPRODUCTION

How and where should we store our resources? To what extent should students have free access to them? Different media pose different problems, so it is difficult to generalise.

We have normally allowed students access to books for independent study and browsing within the school library, and home reading has been encouraged by book loans. In some schools students are obliged to borrow books. The value of 'compulsory library use' may be questioned but few of us, on the other hand, would sympathise with the headmaster who was heard to telephone a member of staff, 'Why have I just found three of your girls on their way to the library – you know it is locked every afternoon!'

The relative remoteness of the centralised library from the classroom has to some extent inhibited the use of books for reference. A significant result of the rise in enquiry-based methods has been the fragmentation of the central library as departments have withdrawn on a temporary basis the books they needed on chosen topics to support the resources already gathered and prepared. This has avoided a constant movement of students across the school. Within the department reference or resource area subject classification and grouping of topic materials can be a simpler problem. The department resource area developed successfully before arguments arose for a central resource area. We shall return to those arguments in the following chapter.

Let us now consider eight different types of non-book material now commonly used in our schools, noting the ways in which they may be handled, stored and reproduced.

Newspaper cuttings

Newspaper cuttings are quite commonly used by teachers in some subjects to provide up-to-date information, evidence or stimulating ideas. For example, statistics for the local area and new information about North Sea oil exploitation can be made available, though they will not be in any textbook.

Cuttings, including colour photos from the Sunday supplements, may be kept in cardboard boxes under broad subjects, ready for selection and editing by staff or use by students.

Where this material is to be made available as individual, indexed items, it is best to stick the cuttings on to A4 paper sheets and treat them as single sheet items.

What we now do with the single sheet depends of course on our reason for obtaining it. If it is to be placed in the central library as a reference item, then it may most conveniently be put in an A4 file as the standard way of displaying single sheet material. If the general retrieval system depends on accession numbers, then the single sheets will have to be filed in order of accession number. It would be better for most purposes, however, if files could be labelled according to the Dewey decimal classification and/or subjects. The files may all be kept on a special shelf in the library but it may be possible as an alternative to locate the files on the relevant book shelf. There may be files for teachers' access only which are stored separately by the librarian.

We may, however, plan to use the item in the classroom. There are several ways of doing this. We may simply hand out the A4 sheets to the students for a set piece of writing or discussion. If we want to make single sheet items available to the students, then we may put them into A4 files or into A4 wallet folders, which can be pinned on the wall. The wallet folders may be used like 'Jackdaws'.

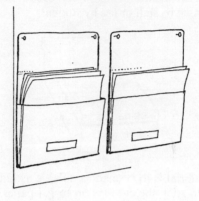

If the sheets are to be used frequently, we can protect them by putting them into plastic wallets or envelopes. This is generally a better alternative to laminating.

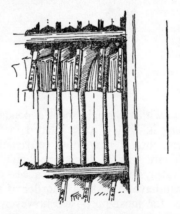

A different storage problem arises if we produce multiple copies for class use and then keep them. The experience of many schools suggests that a suspended filing system such as Railex is the best solution, particularly as it allows the storage of duplicating stencils as well.

This brings us to the question of reproducing the newspaper cutting. The text may of course be typed out, but for facsimile copies we must turn to the electronic scanner stencil or off-set litho for good quality copies. Thermographic stencil copies may be difficult to read unless the typeface is large and clear-cut. For occasional copies a photocopier will suffice. If the cutting is in fact a colour photo, an electronic scanner stencil will give black and white copies but for some purposes a colour slide may be the better solution.

The use of an accession number is really essential at the stage of producing more copies for we need it later to locate the original and the stencil. Originals should be kept in special A4 files for future re-use and checking. Stencils should be stored in accession order number like the multiple copies, and preferably in the same suspended filing unit. The accession number must also be put on the copies.

Reproduction of newspaper cuttings involves copyright clearance, a matter to which we must return later.

Filmstrips

Filmstrips are still widely used in schools, sometimes in conjunction with tape recordings, though slide sets are often preferred because the sequence can be changed.

Once used almost entirely for formal teaching lessons, filmstrips are now made available in some schools for individual and small group reference work. Small plastic viewers using only natural light are cheap and fairly acceptable, but small battery-operated models are now available. Small, cheaper projectors are also available for small group use, using either a rear-projection screen cabinet or simply a dark corner of the classroom.

The filmstrip is relatively expensive and it would be difficult to justify two departments in a school purchasing the same strip. This happens not infrequently, however, where there is no communication between departments or central recording of materials in the school. Whether a filmstrip should normally be stored within a department or in a central resource unit may be determined chiefly by the likely extent of its use. A few schools display filmstrips within the library, giving students open access to them and the necessary viewing facilities. Other schools prefer to hold them in a non-book store with restricted, controlled access.

The storage of filmstrips is not an easy matter. They may be put into the trays of standard metal cabinets and this has the advantage of keeping the notes or booklet that usually accompany the

filmstrip with it. This is an expensive method. It keeps the material dust-free but hides them from view.

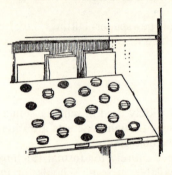

An alternative is to purchase or construct a display/storage shelf which allows booklets to be kept at the back.

The need to reproduce further copies of a filmstrip rarely arises. Strips or slides can be copied with a special camera attachment, or commercial photographic services may be used.

Pamphlet

A pamphlet is a thin paper-covered book with fewer than 20–24 pages, and it may be used at many stages of learning. Although pamphlets or booklets produced within schools may be of A4 size, folded to A5 or about nine by seven inches to match exercise books and allow easier carrying (A4 is too large for most satchels and duffle bags), those produced commercially vary considerably in size. Class sets may conveniently be held in suspended filing but single copies cannot easily be placed among books and may best be contained in open access boxes on shelves with the range of subject content clearly shown. Quite suitable boxes can be made in the school.

A pamphlet which is to be reproduced must be split into its separate pages. If the typeface is reasonably large and clear, without tone pictures, a thermographic stencil may give duplicated copies of an adequate quality. Otherwise an electronic scanner stencil or offset litho process, if available, is required unless the text is retyped. If pages are folded a long-arm stapler will probably be needed. As with single sheet material, accession numbers are necessary to refer to the stencils and the original copy.

Records

Few schools have a large record library. Yet the range of recordings now available commercially, including sound effects, folk music on selected themes, archive music and sound documentaries, is attractive. Cost and lack of playing facilities through the school inhibit the wider use of records. We may see one role of an area or teachers' centre as the holding and lending to schools a comprehensive collection of such scarce resources.

Access to records and record-playing equipment is normally limited to teachers, even just to members of the music department. In resource centres now being built in some school-building programmes, record storage is centralised and the librarian/technician's room has a record deck which is linked to a number of listening positions in the reference area and also to the wiring channels linking all learning areas in the school. In such situations the records are held in a non-book store, on appropriate shelving, though the record sleeve may be displayed within the library.

The problem of playing facilities in a traditional building would be overcome if copyright were not infringed in making a tape copy of a record. This would also reduce the likelihood of damage to the record in use. Copyright enquiries should be sent to the recording company or the British Record Producers Association, Blythe Road, Hayes, Middlesex.

Slides

Slides are a popular resource, both for formal instruction and enquiry-based methods. Most educational slides are of 35 mm size. As for filmstrips, small individual viewers, made of plastic and relying on natural light, can be used, and there is a range of small viewers which operate on batteries or mains power. Small projectors allow small groups to view a larger image, while classroom projectors (and those for lecture theatres with long-throw lenses) can be obtained with slide magazines for easier operation.

The cheapest viewers give little or no magnification but are convenient for many learning situations. A small projection bay is easily made in a room with a table and white sheet of paper on a wall or pinboard screen, providing an electric socket is available. Dim-out may be contrived for a small bay without great difficulty.

A room used chiefly for projecting visual aids needs no natural light and the windows could be blacked out, though consideration must then be given to ventilation. A fixed projection point is advisable. Those of us who have laboured amid a spaghetti of wiring know the advantage of ducted lines. A wired system can be installed cheaply, given the technical knowledge. Where there is a will there is usually a way.

One question arising with slides is whether they should be stored as individual items or in sets. Most occasions in school involve a set of slides on a particular topic, the number in a set varying from six to fifty.

For individual and group work, slides can be made available in a slide box. These normally contain fifty or a hundred numbered sections for slides. The plastic containers holding twenty or thirty-six, which the photographic firms use to send slides to customers, can be used, and cost nothing. In either case information about the slide must either be written on the slide itself or given on an accompanying sheet of paper which may be inconvenient to store afterwards.

A plastic wallet may be used, which has the advantage of showing notes above the pocketed slides, and these may be viewed together. Students may thus examine the slides without touching them at all and remove them only if they are to be projected. A wallet

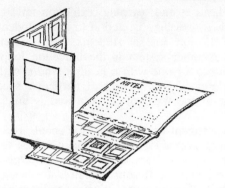

opening out to A4 size may hold twelve to sixteen slides and some schools prepare their slide sets with this format in mind. If wallets have a tab at the side they may be held in A4 files or in suspended filing. Otherwise they may be put in drawers. Larger plastic wallets may be obtained to hold twenty, twenty-four or thirty-six slides. Some versions have a pocket for information notes. They are stored in suspended filing. Large sets only used for instructional purposes in the same sequence could be stored in magazines ready for projection.

It is an advantage to obtain copies of good slides owned by teachers or visitors. Unless the school or a member of staff has the right attachment for a 35 mm camera, it is necessary to use a commercial service at greater cost. Slide copying is another facility which we might expect at an area or regional centre.

Tapes

Tape recorders using tape spools are much in demand in schools but many teachers prefer the tape cassette with its recorder, which is easier to operate. Where a cassette player alone is used without recording facilities, the tape is further protected from accidental spoiling.

Tape is used for formal teaching but its most systematic use is in the teaching of languages. Schools still rely heavily on commercially produced courses. Tape is also a valuable resource in enquiry-based group work and it is in this area perhaps that teachers have been most active in making their own tape-recordings.

The acoustics of the average secondary school classroom are far from ideal and unless the more sophisticated equipment of a language lab is available, listening is more effective as a small group activity. The headset and 'earplug' extension now allow tapes to be played without causing distraction to other students. A junction box makes it possible for six students with headsets to listen to one machine. Another system is the induction loop which offers listening facility to anyone with a headset who is within the circuit of the wired loop. This is a wire of particular specification, run round the top of the walls of a room and is linked into a tape player.

Within a department or a library, tape spools and cassettes may be left with open access for students but it is best to have playing facilities close by. Some librarians screw cassette players to a desk top in a supervised area. Resource centres are being planned with a tape deck, in the librarian's room, wired to listening positions and to other learning areas. The latter facility might be used by individual students starting a new foreign language in their independent study periods.

Tape spools and cassettes can be stored in open racks, shelves with vertical slatting or metal tray cabinets. The box for each spool or cassette needs to bear a clear description of the recording.

Recordings can be duplicated or transferred between spool and cassette by linking the input/output sockets of two machines. The appropriate wire and plugs are necessary and technical advice may be required. Much use is made of off-air recording of educational broadcasts within the limits imposed by the BBC since the timetable need not then be geared to broadcasting times. Timeclocks can be used to save technicians' time.

Videotapes

The purchase of videotape-recorders has placed some schools in a dilemma because the high cost of videotape has precluded the building of an extensive library, even where copyright problems have been overcome. The acquisition of a camera to allow the creative use of videotape has aggravated the financial problem.

Videotape may become cheaper as it is more commonly used. On the other hand a change-over to video cassettes might bring some of the confusion that has reigned over dual standards in 8 mm loop cassettes.

The expense and relative sophistication of the videotape machine is likely to restrict its educational use. The tapes are most likely to be stored on shelves in a non-book store with restricted access. The copying of videotape relies on the two machines involved being compatible and this is unlikely to be the case unless a common buying policy has been adopted in the LEA. This is in fact easily justified on the grounds of efficient maintenance services and the possibility of establishing an area recording and library service.

Wallcharts

Are wallcharts fully exploited as teaching and reference resources? If not, and if they are sometimes treated as wallpaper, it may be because of the difficulties in storing them. Rolls of charts may be seen in tea chests, umbrella stands and wine racks but these are unsightly and the charts easily damaged. Charts do not lie easily in map chest drawers, often because they come to the school rolled in a tubular container, and the same shortcoming applies to other horizontal storage. There is the added difficulty of retrieving one chart from a large number.

Vertical storage is the most effective. An architect's plan file can hold up to 500 charts, any one of which can be extracted individually without bother. Reference is easily made to accession numbers or subjects. At about £100, however, it is not a cheap solution and an efficient unit on the same lines could be made by a school's technical department for a small fraction of the sum.

COPYRIGHT

Communications technology has led us to invest authority in a wider, and more accessible, range of media, requiring us to reassess the traditional role of the teacher and the textbook author and encouraging us to use more materials and sources.

This situation brings us to the problem of copyright. Copyright is defined under our laws as the exclusive right to do, and to authorise other persons to do, certain acts in relation to a literary, dramatic, artistic or musical work. Among these acts is copying. An explicit statement will be found at the front of newly published books that 'No part of this publication may be reproduced, stored in a retrieval system, or transmitted in any form, or by any means, electronic, mechanical, photocopying, recording, or otherwise, without prior permission of the Copyright owner.' ('Retrieval system' in this context refers to computer print-out facilities.)

Our laws on copyright are reasonably specific but they are consistently broken in our schools. 'Where ignorance is bliss, 'Tis folly to be wise.'

We want to reproduce materials quickly and cheaply for good educational reasons. The authors and producers of copyright material naturally wish to protect their livelihood. This conflict is enshrined in no less a document than the Universal Declaration of Human Rights, which in Article 27 says both:

'Everyone has the right freely to participate in the cultural life of the community, to enjoy the arts and to share in scientific advancement and its benefits.'

and:

'Everyone has the right to the protection of the moral and material interest resulting from any scientific, literary or artistic production of which he is the author.'

British law states that we may not copy without prior permission any work subject to copyright.[26] In the case of books this covers the text, illustrations and typography. Copyright lasts for fifty years after the death of an author or, in the case of some audio-visual works such as television programmes and films, fifty years after the date of registration or publication. In practice the addition of © with the name of the copyright owner and date is sufficient to establish copyright on material. Copyright on typography lasts for twenty-five years, even where the text or music itself is not subject to copyright. Museums may claim copyright on photocopies they supply of archive materials.

The position however gives a little flexibility in that certain exceptions, or 'fair dealings', are allowed. Thus *single* copies may be made of extracts of up to 4,000 words for the purpose of 'private study', though this should not exceed 10 per cent of the whole work and therefore excludes poems and other short works. Up to 800 words may be used for a criticism or review.

To copy a class set of material subject to copyright certainly obliges us by law to obtain the permission of the copyright owner. Those who do this at present find that authors and publishers are generous and helpful, and payment is not normally demanded. Yet an impossible situation would arise if every school were to follow the law to the letter. Discussions are being conducted at national level to explore ways of copying material in schools which are fair to both main parties. Again we must look outside the individual school and it may be that Local Authorities or regional centres will be asked to pay an annual fee on the basis of the metered or assessed use of copyright materials by schools in their area.

At present the acknowledgement on school-copied material *Reproduced by Courtesy of Any Publisher Ltd* causes what might be known as the 'halo effect'.

Chapter 4

Resource Areas and Services

THE SECONDARY SCHOOL RESOURCE CENTRE

There are two main roles for a school resource centre. One concerns management, in the efficient ordering, classifying, indexing, storing, displaying, retrieving, lending and maintenance of material and information. The second role concerns the active production of resources through curriculum development.

I am going to assume here, on the basis of arguments already stated, that a resource centre should grow from the base of the existing library and that it will link and serve a number of resource areas in faculties or departments around the school. The relationship between the departmental resource areas and the central unit needs to be determined before the latter can be considered in any detail. The emerging pattern appears to be a central unit which holds those resources and pieces of equipment that are not used exclusively in one department area and makes them available to departments on request, while holding a central index of all resources existing in the school and its neighbourhood.

Conflicts inevitably arise when centralisation is being considered. Facilities such as a dark room and recording room are not easily won in a school and there is a strong argument for making them centrally available to all staff, and perhaps students, though departments using them most regularly may complain of inconvenience and be very reluctant to surrender equipment already in use.

Maintenance of equipment is facilitated by the central holding of those items which are not in full-time use in particular departments. On the other hand the more equipment is moved, the more it is likely to need maintenance.

The pooling of departmental resources which are not by their nature unique to a particular department makes more material available to all. But this advantage will not be accepted by those who protect their authority in departmental mysteries and autonomy. In some school buildings the distances involved in visiting a central unit might add weight to their criticisms. Reaction tends to refer to teaching materials. The location of reference materials will be determined more by the methods being employed and by the age of the students. In schools where older students are given generous time for independent study and have been encouraged to use a library or study hall, centralised materials may be heavily used. Many teachers, particularly of the lower years, develop their enquiry-based projects and subjects within fairly clearly prescribed limits which make it feasible for the necessary resources to be contained for that period in the room or department area. This greater stability is welcomed by those who advocate a greater continuity from primary schooling to the secondary school and who place importance upon the social skills and group behaviour in learning.

Within these broad terms, let us examine the possible design, staffing and financing of a school resource centre.

The planning of a main school resource centre should consider the need for:

main library/resource learning area,
small room for AVA group work,
recording room,
dark room,
librarian's room,
non-book store,
reprographics room,
maintenance bay,
staff work area,

   and possibly
a careers suite.

The relative sizes of these physical needs demand careful examination, as does the relationship between them. The following plan shows an Oxfordshire design which came from close consultation between architect, the school and advisers. The space allocated in this eight-form entry, 11–16 school is approximately:

main library/resource area 140 sq. metres,
recording room 7 sq. metres,
dark room (already existing in near-by science centre),
librarian's room 13 sq. metres,
non-book store 16 sq. metres,
reprographics room and resource officer 18 sq. metres,
staff work area (team) 10 sq. metres,
careers suite (existing nearer main school entrance).

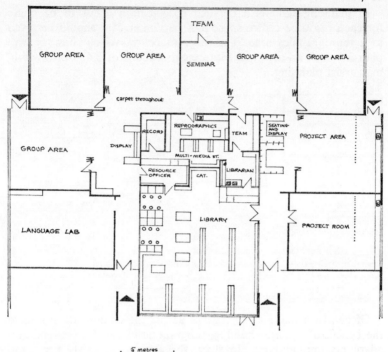

It would be very difficult indeed to expand these areas under existing cost limits without absorbing space which has been time-tabled under traditional school policies. In other words the facilities can only be increased by taking timetabled areas from elsewhere in the school and using 'independent study' to reduce the timetabling load.

In the illustrated plan the language laboratory is included as a more centralised scarce resource, while a number of learning spaces have been grouped around the resource centre to give more direct access and the possibility of future expansion.

The main library area includes twelve carrels which are wired to tape and record desks in the librarian's room. More informal fur-niture is used in the part of the library most likely to be used for leisure reading. An important feature not shown on this plan is the AVA/lecture theatre for 120+ students which lies across a small courtyard from the resource centre. All learning areas are fed by wiring with radio and television channels. Most of the spaces shown are carpeted, primarily to reduce sound levels.

*

In planning schools a detailed specification needs to be made for each resource centre space and particular care should be given to a reprographics area. The diagram below, which shows a wall plan for such an area, split into eight sections of 2,400 mm width, may assist planning.

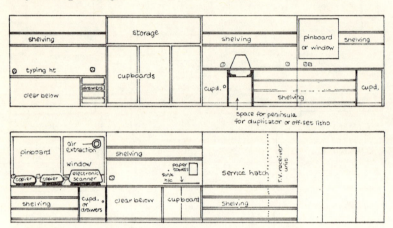

Of course a majority of schools across the country do not have the benefit of a major building programme in which to extend and adapt accommodation. However, the same area exists per pupil of the same group; indeed, schools built in the 1950s are likely to have more. It is a matter of attitudes rather than space.

The opportunity to create a resource centre much larger than the existing library may not be appreciated until the need to restructure the school's organisation is recognised. The establishing of a full, working resource centre implies no less than this.

How, for example, should the centre be financed? Is it reasonable to establish a system for debiting each department for each item of material it consumes? A medium-sized school may duplicate half a million sheets a year; it is certainly the experience of schools that the purchase of reprographic equipment can treble or quadruple stationery bills. In one such school 80 per cent of the ancillary staff's time and supplies were taken by the History department alone. A policy adopted in some schools has been to put 20 per cent or 30 per cent of the total annual capitation into a resource centre account before allocations are made to departments. Departments may then be debited only for spending over a certain limit. Another alternative is to make the resource centre the purchasing agency for the whole school.

The staffing of a resource centre again turns us to the wider school situation. As in many Local Authorities the setting-up of a resource centre will not be immediately rewarded with an increase in the ancillary staff, the redeployment and retraining of any technicians, secretaries and helpers already in the school may have to be considered.

The tasks to be performed in the full running of a successful centre fall into five main categories.

First, there is the active involvement of teachers in planning, preparation and curriculum development. This requires professional expertise, though the proportion of teachers genuinely engaged in innovation may be very small. The great amount of time needed for thorough planning and development poses the need for a member of staff to act simply as a replacement – the school's own supply teacher. Some teachers spend more than 800 hours a year outside school hours preparing resources. The expertise and guidance needed in the preparation of resources and courses poses the need for a senior member of staff with the experience and flair to stimulate and advise others in curriculum development. The role might be that of educational manager over the resource centre, advising on learning methods, co-ordinating work between faculties or departments and managing central funds. Both posts may have to be established from within the existing staff structure and neither time nor circumstances may offer an immediate opportunity.

Second, there is the task of designing resources to a good standard. A designer competent in the lay-out of educational materials in a variety of media soon makes his presence felt but schools can rarely afford such specialist services. The quality of products even in regional centres depends very much on the presence of artistic skills and a few teachers' centres, for instance, have gained the co-operation of local art colleges. Fortunate is the school with a helper who has an artistic hand.

Third, there is the task of managing the library service, indexing and classifying, providing information. The role of the school librarian has been outlined in the Library Association's recommended standards for policy and provision in school library resource centres. In fact the schools which have a qualified librarian still represent a small minority but the appointment of a librarian, qualified, sympathetic to the needs of staff and students, aware of the full range of educational resources to be handled, and accepted as a full member of staff, seems almost indispensable to the efficient working of a resource centre.

Fourth, there are the technical skills needed for the smooth running of equipment and first-line maintenance. An AVA technician exists in some schools; technical assistance is important to the successful operation of a language laboratory. A technician could combine, in some cases, AVA assistance with duties in science labs and workshops.

Fifth, and lastly, clerical and secretarial skills are necessary for the typing, duplicating and many other office tasks. Since the reprographics areas of a centre may draw together the duplicating and printing facilities for the whole school, and much of the typing, it is reasonable to ask whether some of the traditional school office staff should not be transferred there. The school administration area is then concerned more with school correspondence and records.[27]

In appointing ancillary staff, personality, initiative, the readiness to retrain and the ability to work harmoniously with others are often counted more important than qualifications. It is unlikely that schools will be able to employ the range of ancillary staff they feel they need. Outward-looking schools have attracted the freely given services of local parents and this is admirable. The voluntary help of students, within or outside lesson times, has also been advocated but this is more open to criticism.

A working party in one Local Authority looked at the management of school resource centres and suggested the following staff structure in a school of 1,000 students. It was accepted that this scale of provision could not be achieved locally in the near future.[28]

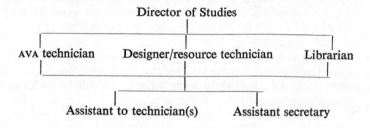

Director of Studies

AVA technician   Designer/resource technician   Librarian

Assistant to technician(s)   Assistant secretary

THE FACULTY RESOURCE AREA IN USE

The faculty or department resource area is a range of facilities shared by a number of teaching spaces and preferably additional to them. It is a means of making resources more directly available to students working in the faculty and if the area is not itself a teaching space the problem of interruption to formal lessons can be avoided.

In traditional school planning five rooms were often provided for the equivalent of four classes, the fifth room being used for split groups but more often standing empty because this was the margin deemed necessary for timetabling.

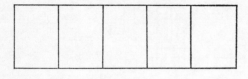

What has happened in school building programmes in an increasing number of Authorities is that the equivalent of the fifth area has been adopted as a shared resource area and it has been increased with an element of circulation space.

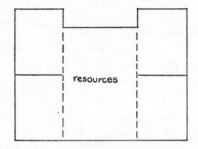

This pattern is well suited to resource-based learning and co-operative teaching. The relationships between the class areas and the resource area may be determined chiefly by noise levels; for instance, a carpeted area with no practical facilities might be openly related to the resource area by a wide opening or a movable screen. A space for practical activities, with sinks and working surfaces, might be enclosed by a door. On the other hand one formal, carpeted room might be enclosed for formal teaching purposes and this space would have first priority for black-out.

This basic plan can be applied to many departments.

In the 11–13 study centres shown (p. 88), up to 240 students can be accommodated for a broad range of group activities. The two resource areas, which can be opened up to each other, are intended for independent study and can hold both book and non-book materials. Though part of an 11–16 comprehensive, it is not unlike some middle school situations. In these central areas built-in furniture allows for exhibitions, though some of the most successful

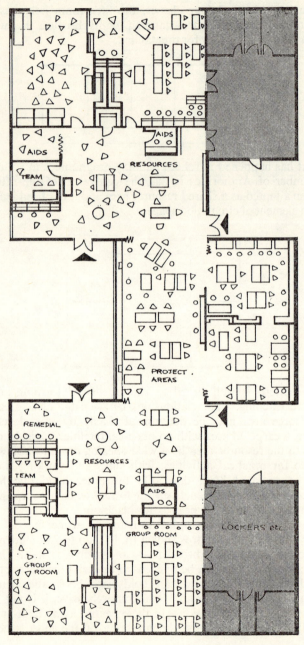

displays are in practice created with boxes to give different levels, coloured drapes and rolls of corrugated cardboard. A small, enclosed aids room provides facilities for viewing visual aids and making tapes, though difficulties have arisen under current cost limits in achieving both ventilation and sound insulation. A bay is provided for remedial work – a deliberate attempt in planning to integrate students having learning problems with their peer group by giving them specialist aids and tutoring within their own study centre. This whole unit of accommodation is used by some schools in one Authority for Humanities, Mathematics and Foreign Language studies, and the remedial bay is manned at certain times by a mobile remedial specialist.

We might in planning consider an inversion of the above plan, placing the practical facilities in the central spaces.

The following diagram illustrates an 11–14 science centre where

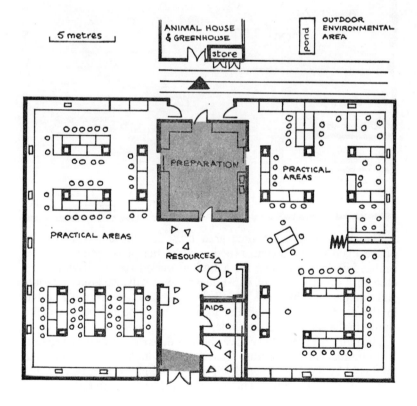

a central space accommodates a reference area. In Science resources must be taken to include the equipment and materials held in the preparation room, and this too is centralised, operating a trolley and hatch service to the learning areas. It is unlikely that these materials would be shown on lists outside the department.

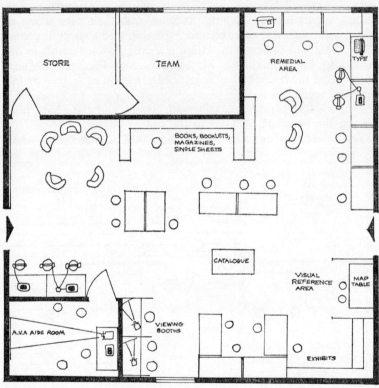

The departmental resource area must be considered a satellite of the main resource centre to the extent that it is serviced by the centre, holding and using for a limited period resources which are otherwise stored centrally. Most departments will also hold materials and equipment which are in full-time use and are normally stored in the department, though the location of some of these may be shown in the school's central index.

The more detailed plan above shows a department resource shared by four adjacent classrooms. The equipment indicated represents the total held by the department itself and its use in this area by students is flexible and economic. The equipment, like the materials, may of course move into classrooms for certain purposes, mainly instructional. Such an area is what one might expect for the resource centre in a 9–13 middle school, with the team room being used for reprographics.

Within a faculty area we may consider it worthwhile to have on display only those resources which are relevant to current courses of study, though these could be wide-ranging for work which is student-centred or where many age groups use the same facilities.

Need a faculty have its own indexing and cataloguing system? It depends on the scale of the problem. A tidy and well-labelled stock of cardboard boxes might be adequate together with an efficient stock book. A distinction may have to be made between what the faculty has stored, which teachers may require to know, and what resources are available on a study topic, which students may want to ascertain.

Let us at this point look at five actual situations within schools to observe differences in practice.

Situation 1

The first example is not perhaps an exemplary one, though Mr X is a good teacher. He works, like other members of the History department, in isolation and teaches for most of the week in his own room, running his History courses with the books allocated by his head of department. Mr X is a passionate historian and communicates his rapture to his students. He tries to make imaginative use of tape-recordings, photocopies of archive material, 'colour supplement' pictures and articles, and his own spirit-duplicated worksheets. However, Mr X's stock cupboard is something of a school legend and the last cleaning lady who inadvertently opened the door was so bruised around the ankles by the avalanche of material that she refused to enter the room again. His lack of organisation in fact prevents him from taking full advantage of his own industry and drives him back more frequently than he would like to the standard textbooks – and even these seem to disappear mysteriously. His headmaster refers to him rather unkindly as 'Ethelred the Unready'.

Situation 2

As we walk into the second situation, a middle school, about 150 eleven-year-olds are working in a suite of spaces which encourage a variety of activities, including experimental Science and Art and

Craft. The students spend the greater part of the week in this, their home base. They move across to the facilities they need and though there are some periods of formal class work, at this point they are engaged on studies arising from a visit to a local quarry. About a dozen students are using the resources of the large Science bay with the assistance of the specialist tutor to make tests upon the rocks they have brought back. Other students are using the Art and Craft area to paint scenes around the quarry and two are drawing diagrams of fossils. Three boys are trying their hand at stone carving in the outside courtyard. (There is an external work area in this school which includes a pond, an aviary, a courtyard for practical work and an environmental corner for ecological studies.) A number of students are writing about their experience and a few are composing poems.

In the shared resource area or library some children are examining the photographs, tools and quarrymen's clothes which have been lent by the local museum service and which offer evidence of the quarry when it was being worked some forty years ago. At a map table two boys are making their own maps with the help of Ordnance Survey maps. A small group are still completing a previous project on 'The Sea'.

The books to which students refer are laid out on shelves in broad Dewey numbering with both the numbers and subjects clearly shown. The teachers, led by their Year Tutor, have gathered the fiction which has some connection with quarrying, stone, mining and geology, and these books are displayed with an inviting notice in a prominent position.

Next to the book shelves is a shelved bay containing A4 boxes. Each box bears its topic title and Dewey relationship. These boxes contain non-book materials and the contents are shown on the inside of the hinged lid. The boxes cover the topics likely to be tackled during the school year and they are an attempt to anticipate and stimulate student interests.

The teachers are not immediately to be seen in this situation for they are helping individuals and small groups.

The middle school has four suites of accommodation like this, one for each age group. Each holds a list of the resources held by the others and there is some interchange.

Situation 3

The third situation again involves 11–12-year-olds of mixed ability but this time in the First Year of an 11–16 comprehensive. Three class groups are blocked for the full morning with their tutors for Humanities, though this is the only time in the week when the timetable allows this blocking. The rooms are adjacent and have doors on to a corridor which has a screened resources bay which the school itself converted from a coat-hanging space. A hall near by is available for drama.

The topic for this half-term is survival on an island which each group of four students has already created and located on the basis of chosen geological, climatic and ecological criteria. Evidence for models was drawn from books and filmstrips linked to prepared tapes.

The survival topic began when the party going to study the islands was 'lost in a plane ditching at sea'. An extract from 'The Lord of the Flies' led into role-play situations and last week the survival officer from the local Air Force station came to talk on his subject, showed a film and demonstrated equipment – a resounding success.

The groups' enquiries are based first on a study guide which confronts them with problems in terms of their chosen island environment and their own locality. This study guide and the booklet of information on human and animal survival in three climatic zones (a necessary first source of information as no commercial publication meets the need, especially for the less able) were produced by one of the teachers involved in co-operation with colleagues from three other schools – one of a number of joint curriculum development ventures. She is a married woman with three children of her own at school and she works closely with her own school colleagues to exploit these jointly devised materials, which were printed at the area teachers' centre. She has a deep interest in the children and the school as a social community and gives a great deal of her life to the school. Her husband, in higher education, has suggested that she is 'too professional'. Because team-work enthuses the whole school there has been none of the common reaction by other departments against team-teaching and enquiry methods. At the back of the school the Biologist employs the same group-work methods in projects, a major part of which is devoted to original investigations of animal behaviour – living resources. The Foreign Language department uses many audio-visual materials to teach French to all students in the school in mixed ability groups.

For the Humanities work the basic booklets are supported by reference books, exhibits, slides and selected fiction, some of the latter ordered from the schools' library service. The books and exhibits are shelved in the resources bay across the corridor and shared by the three classes when blocked. The audio-visual aids are held in one room under the supervision of a teacher. Most of the materials available are mentioned in the students' study guide and a simple card index in the resources bay mentions them all and their location.

Situation 4

In our fourth situation twenty-five Sixth Year students are taking General Studies. The teachers who individually take these studies in the Sixth and Seventh Years decided to spend their allowance on some of the topic packs published by the Schools Council Humanities project and the York General Studies project. The teachers have added a few items of their own but their involvement is limited, they feel, by their commitments, including A-Level courses, elsewhere. The material has all been put on to an optical co-incidence index by one enthusiast. Both the History master and the students now in the general studies room may refer to the index, which is brought out for these periods but is otherwise stored in the cupboard with the materials. Only limited use is made of the library some distance away. The materials are used to stimulate and support discussion.

Situation 5

The last example is in an old Horsa building where three teachers are co-operating in running a Mode III CSE course in Social Sciences. Considerable use is made of film and outside speakers and these are chosen with discretion. At the moment the students are midway through a two-week topic on racial problems. After the general introduction the students chose a case study, for which material was specially prepared on the USA, South Africa and Britain. Mr Y has played the dominant part of devising and preparing this course, which attracts a majority of students from the full range of ability; indeed, he did it almost single-handed over a period of four years and in addition to his other school responsibilities. His dedication has earned the support of colleagues who work in his teams. He reckons he has spent several thousand hours of his own time in course preparation and revision, and even took materials away on his family summer holidays, yet he considers his labours have been worthwhile. The course investigates aspects of human and animal behaviour, and the latter involves several visits to zoos. He has written much of the material and many tape cassettes have been made, some of them linked to the duplicated material, to assist students with reading difficulties. Mr Y says that he would not need to work so hard if he were starting the course now because so many more materials are available from one source or another. But because of his Herculean efforts the small group methods work smoothly and continuous assessment for CSE is based on firm criteria which require evidence of the various skills of obtaining and handling ideas and of making and justifying judgements.

The old, sub-standard Horsa block in which these studies are undertaken has been 'knocked about' and redecorated by the school. The central lobby has been converted to a shared area and here the selection of books are put out for the topic being studied. Booklet and single sheet material is obtained freely from suspended filing cabinets in which each pocket is labelled. A list of slides, filmstrips and cassette tapes is displayed and these items, with the equipment – battery-operated slide and strip viewers, and cassette players, can be obtained from one of the teachers present.

Mr Y, who can now stand back and give his assistance to those students who most need it, has undoubtedly been supported in this approach by the preceding three years in which all students follow an interdisciplinary Humanities course. There is a logical and well-developed continuity of method and resource use.

The school's current extension programme includes a resource centre with the full range of facilities and Mr Y is now considering how much of his material should be placed in the resources centre, which will stand about eighty paces away. He shares this problem with the head of History in a near-by school who uses the same learning approach and finds himself in much the same situation.

Mr Y has no doubts however over the value of a full-blooded production unit, which the headmaster has promised to staff, realistically, for this should bring a much higher standard of presentation to his materials.

THE REGIONAL RESOURCE CENTRE

No school is an island, though some appear to strive to be so. We cannot argue that as schools we are in any real way self-reliant and self-sufficient. Most of our materials and equipment come from external sources and we constantly take advantage of the ideas, facilities and services that are found beyond our walls.

In looking beyond the school it may be helpful to distinguish between a region, which is interpreted here as the new local government unit, and an area within a region which is probably served by a teachers' centre and still includes a considerable number of schools.

For what reasons may we look outside the school to the region?

(i) We may wish to look at the resources devised by curriculum development groups in the region and by those produced within individual schools by gifted colleagues and teams. This dissemination of ideas and materials needs an exchange and mart system to do systematically what the best Local Authority advisers have always attempted to do in their own specialist area. A few teachers' centres have undertaken this role and it can stem from the even more valuable action of bringing practitioners together. The dissemination of the best of local practice has been counted important in discussions of regional centres.[29]

(ii) We value information on the sources and expertise that are readily available to us in the region. Can we justify each school undertaking the same search alone? A regional centre can effectively gather such information and put it directly into schools. Does, for example, a local museum have any medieval domestic objects for loan or to study on a visit? Is there a speaker willing, qualified and recommended to talk about drug addiction? Is there a well-documented section of canal worth visiting? Has anyone in the region a set of slides to hire or sell on primitive masks?

This information can be indicated to our schools in several ways but it is important that it should be immediately accessible and not a phone call or letter away.

An area or regional centre can produce a catalogue to indicate the sources, courses and scarce resources (chiefly audio-visual aids) available and their location. A card catalogue could be integrated with the school's resource centre catalogue or developed beside it. Alternatively a printed booklet could be issued, though this is more difficult to keep up to date unless computer banking and print-out facilities are on hand.

It is hardly feasible to include individual books in such a cataloguing service, for the main Authority library supplying schools could hold well over a quarter of a million different titles. This information can only be made available on demand and should be held in a full regional catalogue held in the regional centre and teachers' centres. Developments at national level may lead to computer print-out lists of audio-visual aids on specified topics. Regional centres with suitable facilities would be in a position to handle this information and give it on demand. We must ask ourselves, however, whether it is better to have a film list of one or three hundred. Our needs may have to be described very specifically.

The dissemination of information concerning the teachers' professional role raises rather different questions and this information may best be handled by Teachers' and Professional Centres.

(iii) We want to obtain particular materials. Sometimes, of course, these are simply requisitioned from the commercial publishers or producers. Should we consider the regional centre as a purchasing agency which puts the ordered books and audio-visual aids into schools with index cards ready made for the catalogue? This role has been suggested. But could it be efficient?

The regional distribution of the resource agencies such as the schools' library service, museum services, AVA libraries, teachers' centre resources, archives, charities, firms and institutions will in some cases still be widely dispersed. Local government reorganisation may, at least initially, have increased the number of agencies. Consideration must be given to how some of these may be centralised and the first practical step is to co-ordinate the provision through a joint non-book catalogue as already mentioned.

(iv) Material can be borrowed from many of the sources above. Would it be helpful if such items came to the school with an index card so that its presence in the school could be indicated in the resource centre for that period? Such cards would need a colour coding or alternative signal so that they could quickly be removed and returned with the loan items. This is indeed done in a few areas.

A regional centre could hold and lend to schools the materials produced by Schools Council national projects and other regional projects, affording for the first time a network for dissemination of curriculum development projects.

(v) Those of us who participate in local projects and course workshops want to see materials designed and reproduced to a high quality. Should a region not have a full reprographic centre with the design staff and better printing facilities which our schools individually cannot afford?

(vi) Our equipment in schools needs to be serviced and repaired. Technicians within schools and those providing a general service to schools from teachers' centres can provide 'first-line' maintenance. But what beyond that? Should a region have centralised maintenance services? There appear to be strong economic arguments for this.

(vii) We must by law obtain permission to make copies of material which is subject to copyright. This problem too might find its solution in regional terms. An area and regional centre is bound to do this and it can do so for the schools it serves. It remains however a time-consuming obligation. A regional assessment or metering of copyright 'usage' might be acceptable, though responsibility may fall directly upon the Authority rather than the centre.

Now let us look at the area or teachers' centre. What can it do to meet these needs? It can:

Disseminate information on our role as teachers.

Bring teachers together to discuss, evaluate and make resources.

Hold a copy of a full regional catalogue and help to interpret the needs and demands of local teachers.

Hold resources relevant to the area environment.

Provide workshop facilities.

Advise school staff on the handling and use of resources.

Provide a general AVA equipment and technical service to its schools.

Advise on the methodology of curriculum development.

And now the regional centre. What is it?

The regional centre need not be a single physical entity. It should comprise those main agencies within the region which make resources available to schools and which agree to co-ordinate by contributing their information to a regional catalogue, the non-book section of which can be put into every school. Good arguments can of course be put forward for bringing as many of these agencies as possible into one physical centre.

The regional centre will most reasonably be situated at the schools' library headquarters, which can be expanded to hold available audio-visual aid libraries and perhaps a museum service, and where the main expertise in indexing, classifying, and retrieving materials may be found. A materials production unit and equipment maintenance service might also be sited here.

The core of its constituent parts is the information-handling unit controlling and producing the non-book and full regional catalogue. This calls for standard procedures within the region.

There are dangers in discussing this regional network simply in terms of institutions and their roles. It is people who count. A resource centre, be it within a school or an area, should exist primarily to make us all more resourceful. Its value will be judged finally by the quality of the interactions between teacher and student,

student and student, resources and student which it promotes or facilitates.

It is imperative that there is feed-back from the school to those involved in designing, supplying and advising on resources. This communication calls for dialogue and good personal relationships. Teacher, librarian, adviser – we can too easily seize upon resources and build them up around us till they become a barrier to human contact, separating us rather than bringing us together. There will be hierarchies of organisation but these should not pin us within our institutions.

It is easy too to gain satisfaction from getting and storing resources; there is after all a squirrel inside every good teacher. But they are aids, not an end.

The most important resources of all remain ourselves and our students, for it is in the quality of their experience, their ideas and their response that our ultimate success or failure will be judged.

Notes and References

1. 'Innovation and Stress', *Times Educational Supplement* article based on Lawrence Stenhouse's address (19.1.73).
2. *Children and Their Primary Schools*, Report of the Central Advisory Council of Education (England) (HMSO, 1967).
3. C. B. Cox and A. E. Dyson (eds), *Fight for Education* – a Black Paper (The Critical Quarterly Society, 1969).
4. *Ideas*, a journal published by Goldsmith's College, University of London. See especially Nos 1, 4, 5 and 6.
5. L. C. Taylor, *Resources for Learning* (Penguin, 1971).
6. *The Middle Years of Schooling from 8 to 13*, Working Paper No. 22 (The Schools Council, HMSO, 1969).
7. *Half our Future*, Report of the Central Advisory Council for Education (England) (HMSO, 1963).
8. K. Evans, 'Multi-media Resource Centres: A Cautionary Note', *Secondary Education Journal*, Vol. 1, No. 3 (1971).
9. *Cataloguing of Non-book Materials*, Working Paper No. 6 (National Committee for Educational Technology, 1971).
10. R. Hodgkin, 'The Qualitative Element', *Trends in Education*, No. 29 (HMSO, 1973).
11. Cited in Quillen and Hanna, *Educating for Social Competence* (Scott, Foreman and Co., 1948).
12. See *The Humanities Project – An Introduction* (Heinemann, 1970).
13. Schools Council Working Paper No. 39, *Social Studies 8–13* (Evans/Methuen, 1971).
14. B. S. Bloom *et al.*, *A Taxonomy of Educational Objectives* (McKay, Vol. 1 1956, Vol. 2 1964).
15. *Science 5–13 – Teachers Guide* (Macdonald, Trial Edition, 1972), and 'An Interim Statement', Schools Council Project in History, Geography and Social Science 8–13.
16. For a number of examples see Schools Council Curriculum Bulletin No. 3, *Changes in Schools Science Teaching* (Evans/Methuen, 1970).
17. H. Pankhurst, *Education on the Dalton Plan* (Dutton, 1950).
18. J. Lloyd Trump, *Images of the Future – A New Approach to the Secondary School* (Ford Foundation, 1959).

Resources for Instruction
19. From C. Laye, *The African Child* (Fontana, 1959).
20. Further reading, J. Leedham and D. Unwin, *Programmed Learning in the Schools* (Longmans, 1965).
21. P. J. Tansey and D. Unwin, *Simulation and Gaming in Education* (Methuen, 1969).

Resources for Problem-solving

22. G. and P. Perry, *Case Studies in Adolescence* (Pitman, 1970). Note also their *Case Studies in Teaching* (Pitman).

Designing Resources

23. Further reading: J. Young, *Reprographics Made Easy*, NCAVAE

Classifying and Indexing for Retrieval

24. Further reading: J. Riddle *et al.*, *Non-Book Materials – the Organisation of Integrated Collections* (Canadian Library Association, 1970).
25. Schools Council Working Paper 43: *School Resource Centres* (Evans/Methuen, 1972). Further reading: M. Shiffrin, *Information in the School Library* (Clive Bingley, 1973).

Copyright

26. For further detail:
    'Photocopying and the Law', Publishers Association.
    R. F. Whale, *Copyright* (Longman, 1971).

The School Resource Centre

27. Schools Council, *School Resource Centres: Working Paper 43* (Evans/Methuen, 1972).
28. Further reading:
    Resources and their Management (Oxfordshire Education Committee, 1971).
    A Resources Centre . . . A State of Mind (Scottish Educational Film Association, 1972).
    M. Holder, 'Setting up a school resource centre', *Resources* (April, 1972).
    School Library Resource Centres: Recommended Standards for Policy and Provision (Library Association, 1970).

The Regional Resource Centre

29. Note: E. Garnett, *Area Resource Centre* (Arnold, 1972).
    Regional resource centres are currently being studied by CET and the Schools Council.

A Selection of Film Sources

Australian News and Information Bureau, Canberra House, Maltravers St, London WC2

BBC TV Enterprises, 25 The Burroughs, Hendon NW4

British Film Institute, Booking Manager, 81 Dean St, London W1

Central Film Library, Govt Building, Bromyard Avenue, London W37 JB

Concord Films, Nacton, Ipswich, IP10 OJZ

Contemporary Films, 14 Soho Sq., London W1

Ealing Scientific, Greycaine Rd, Watford WD2 4PW

Educational and Television Films Ltd, 164 Shaftesbury Ave, London WC2

EFVA, Foundation Film Library, Brooklands House, Weybridge, Surrey

Information Service of India, India House, Aldwych, London WC2

National Film Board of Canada, 1 Grosvenor Sq., London W1

National Audio-visual Aids Library, Paxton Place, Gipsy Rd, London SE27

New Zealand Film Library, New Zealand House, Haymarket, London SW1

Petroleum Films Bureau, 4 Brook St, Hanover Sq., London W1

Rank Film Library, P.O. Box 70, Great West Rd, Brentford, Middlesex

Scottish Central Film Library, 16 Woodside Terrace, Charing Cross, Glasgow, C3

Sound Services Ltd, Wilton Crescent, Merton Park, London SW19

Unilever Film Library, Unilever House, Blackfriars, London EC4

A Selection of Sources of Audio-visual Materials

Aerofilms Ltd, 4 Albemarle St, London W1X 4HR
American Museum in Britain, Claverton Manor, Bath BA2 7BD
Ashmolean Museum, Beaumont St, Oxford
Bodleian Library, Broad St, Oxford
Central Office of Information, Photographic Library, Hercules Rd SE1
Geoslides, 4 Christian Fields, London SW16 3JZ
Imperial War Museum, Lambeth Rd, London SE1
National Gallery, Trafalgar Sq., London SW1
Natural History Museum, Cromwell Rd, London SW7
Science Museum, South Kensington, London SW7
Slide Centre, Portman House, 17 Broderick Rd, London SW17 7D2
Sunday Times Filmstrips, Thomson House, Grays Inn Rd, London WC1
Topic Records Ltd, 27 Nassington Rd, London NW3
Visual Education, the magazine of the National Committee for Audio-
   Visual Aids in Education, published annually in its July issue a
   comprehensive list of sources.

Some Sources of Information and Materials

Banking Information Service, 10 Lombard St, London EC3
British Insurance Association, Public Relations Dept, Aldermay House, Queen St, London EC4
Building Societies Association, 14 Park St, London W1
Catholic Institute for International Relations, 33 Kings St, London WC2
Central Council for Health Education, Tavistock House North, Tavistock Sq., London WC1
Centre for Contemporary European Study (Schools Unit), University of Sussex, Falmer, Brighton BN1 9QZ
Christian Aid, 2 Sloane Gardens, London SW1
Civic Trust, 17 Carlton House Terrace, London SW1Y 5AS
Commonwealth Institute, Kensington High St, London SW7
Community Relations Commission, 10–12 Russell Sq., London WC1
Council for the Protection of Rural England, 4 Hobart Place, London SW11W OHY
Countryside Commission, 1 Cambridge Gate, Regents Park, London
European Community Information Centre, 23 Chesham St, London SW1
Family Planning Association, 27–35 Mortimer St, London W1
Friends of the Earth (UK), 8 King St, London WC2
Freedom from Hunger, 17 Northumberland Ave, London WC2
Help the Aged, Room TES2, 8 Denmark St, London W1A 2AP
Oxfam, 274 Banbury Rd, Oxford
National Council for Social Service, 26 Bedford Sq., London WC1
National Marriage Guidance Council, 78 Duke St, Grosvenor Sq., WC1
National Savings Committee, Education Branch, Freepost, London WC2B 6BR
Royal Society for the Protection of Birds, The Lodge, Sandy, Beds.
Save the Children Fund, 29 Queen Anne's Gate, London SW1
Shelter, 86 The Strand, London WC2R OEQ
TUC, Education Dept, Transport House, Smith Sq., London SW1
UNICEF, New Gallery Centre, 123 Regents St, London W1
United Nations Association, Information Office, 25 Charles St, London W1
United Nations Information Centre, 14 Stratford Place, London W1
United States Information Service, American Embassy, Grosvenor Sq., London W1
VOCAD Education Unit (overseas aid), 25 Parnell House, Wilton Rd, London SW1
War on Want, 2b The Grove, Ealing, London W5
White Fathers (Missionaries) Project Service, Sutton Coldfield

A Selection of Industrial Sources

British Iron and Steel Federation, Steel House, Tothill St, London SW1
British Transport Films, Melbury House, Melbury Terrace, London NW1 6LP
Brooke Bond Oxo Education Service, Leon House, High St, Croydon CR9 1JQ
Butter Information Council, Mercury House, Waterloo Rd, SE1
Cadbury Bros Ltd, Schools Dept, Bournville, Birmingham 20
Ceylon Tea Centre, Education Dept, 22 Regent St, London W1
Cotton Board, Home Trade Dept, 3 Albemarle St, Manchester 3
Gas Council, 6 Gt Chapel St, London W1
National Coal Board, Public Relations Dept, Hobart House, Grosvenor Place, London SW1
National Rubber Bureau, 19 Buckingham St, London WC2
Petroleum Information Bureau, 2–4 Brook St, Hanover Sq., London W1X 2AY
Tate and Lyle Ltd, Educational Aids Bureau, 21 Mincing Lane, London EC3
White Fish Authority, 2 Cursitor St, London EC4
Wool Textile Employer's Council, 55 Well St, Bradford 1

Index